THE ENCYCLOPEDIA OF PSYCHOACTIVE DRUGS

SERIES 1

The Addictive Personality
Alcohol and Alcoholism
Alcohol Customs and Rituals
Alcohol Teenage Drinking
Amphetamines Danger in the Fast Lane
Barbiturates Sleeping Potion or Intoxicant?
Caffeine The Most Popular Stimulant
Cocaine A New Epidemic
Escape from Anxiety and Stress
Flowering Plants Magic in Bloom
Getting Help Treatments for Drug Abuse
Heroin The Street Narcotic
Inhalants The Toxic Fumes

LSD Visions or Nightmares?
Marijuana Its Effects on Mind & Body
Methadone Treatment for Addiction
Mushrooms Psychedelic Fungi
Nicotine An Old-Fashioned Addiction
Over-The-Counter Drugs Harmless or Hazardous?
PCP The Dangerous Angel
Prescription Narcotics The Addictive Painkillers
Quaaludes The Quest for Oblivion
Teenage Depression and Drugs
Treating Mental Illness
Valium and Other Tranquilizers

SERIES 2

Bad Trips
Brain Function
Case Histories
Celebrity Drug Use
Designer Drugs
The Downside of Drugs
Drinking, Driving, and Drugs
Drugs and Civilization
Drugs and Crime
Drugs and Diet
Drugs and Disease
Drugs and Emotion
Drugs and Pain
Drugs and Perception
Drugs and Pregnancy
Drugs and Sexual Behavior

Drugs and Sleep
Drugs and Sports
Drugs and the Arts
Drugs and the Brain
Drugs and the Family
Drugs and the Law
Drugs and Women
Drugs of the Future
Drugs Through the Ages
Drug Use Around the World
Legalization: A Debate
Mental Disturbances
Nutrition and the Brain
The Origins and Sources of Drugs
Substance Abuse: Prevention and Treatment
Who Uses Drugs?

DRUGS & SEXUAL BEHAVIOR

GENERAL EDITOR
Professor Solomon H. Snyder, M.D.
*Distinguished Service Professor of
Neuroscience, Pharmacology, and Psychiatry at
The Johns Hopkins University School of Medicine*

•

ASSOCIATE EDITOR
Professor Barry L. Jacobs, Ph.D.
*Program in Neuroscience, Department of Psychology,
Princeton University*

•

SENIOR EDITORIAL CONSULTANT
Joann Rodgers
*Deputy Director, Office of Public Affairs at
The Johns Hopkins Medical Institutions*

THE ENCYCLOPEDIA OF PSYCHOACTIVE DRUGS
SERIES 2
DRUGS & SEXUAL BEHAVIOR

JOANN ELLISON RODGERS

CHELSEA HOUSE PUBLISHERS
NEW YORK • PHILADELPHIA

On the Cover: *The Kiss* by Edvard Munch

Chelsea House Publishers
EDITOR-IN-CHIEF: Nancy Toff
EXECUTIVE EDITOR: Remmel T. Nunn
MANAGING EDITOR: Karyn Gullen Browne
COPY CHIEF: Juliann Barbato
PICTURE EDITOR: Adrian G. Allen
ART DIRECTOR: Giannella Garrett
MANUFACTURING MANAGER: Gerald Levine

The Encyclopedia of Psychoactive Drugs
SENIOR EDITOR: Jane Larkin Crain

Staff for DRUGS AND SEXUAL BEHAVIOR:
ASSOCIATE EDITOR: Paula Edelson
ASSISTANT EDITOR: Laura-Ann Dolce
COPY EDITOR: James Guiry
DEPUTY COPY CHIEF: Ellen Scordato
EDITORIAL ASSISTANT: Susan DeRosa
ASSOCIATE PICTURE EDITOR: Juliette Dickstein
PICTURE RESEARCHER: Lynn Goldberg
DESIGNER: Victoria Tomaselli
DESIGN ASSISTANT: Laura Lang
PRODUCTION COORDINATOR: Joseph Romano

Copyright © 1988 by Chelsea House Publishers, a division of Main Line Book Co.
All rights reserved. Printed and bound in the United States of America.

3 5 7 9 8 6 4 2

Library of Congress Cataloging in Publication Data
Rodgers, Joann Ellison.
  Drugs and sexual behavior / Joann Rodgers.
  p. cm.—(The Encyclopedia of psychoactive drugs. Series 2)
  Bibliography: p.
  Includes index.
  1. Aphrodisiacs—Juvenile literature. 2. Psychotropic drugs
—Physiological effect—Juvenile literature. 3. Drugs
and sex—Juvenile literature. I. Title. II. Series.
RM386.R63   1988   615'.7—dc19   87-23272
                                         CIP
                                         AC

ISBN 1-55546-215-4
   0-7910-0792-8 (pbk.)

CONTENTS

Foreword 9
Introduction 13
Author's Preface 19
1 Sexual Arousal 23
2 Hormones: Nature's Own Drugs 33
3 Aphrodisiacs: Fact or Fiction? 43
4 Psychoactive Drugs and Sex 51
5 Sexual Problems: Physiological and Psychological 59
6 Legitimate Drug Treatment and Sexual Therapy 67
7 Conclusion 71
Editor's Note 73
Appendix: State Agencies 78
Further Reading 84
Glossary 85
Index 90

Myths about the power of various plants and potions to enhance sex have been in circulation for thousands of years. Even in the 20th century, such hearsay is still eagerly spread by teens and adults alike.

FOREWORD

In the Mainstream of American Life

One of the legacies of the social upheaval of the 1960s is that psychoactive drugs have become part of the mainstream of American life. Schools, homes, and communities cannot be "drug proofed." There is a demand for drugs — and the supply is plentiful. Social norms have changed and drugs are not only available—they are everywhere.

But where efforts to curtail the supply of drugs and outlaw their use have had tragically limited effects on demand, it may be that education has begun to stem the rising tide of drug abuse among young people and adults alike.

Over the past 25 years, as drugs have become an increasingly routine facet of contemporary life, a great many teenagers have adopted the notion that drug taking was somehow a right or a privilege or a necessity. They have done so, however, without understanding the consequences of drug use during the crucial years of adolescence.

The teenage years are few in the total life cycle, but critical in the maturation process. During these years adolescents face the difficult tasks of discovering their identity, clarifying their sexual roles, asserting their independence, learning to cope with authority, and searching for goals that will give their lives meaning.

Drugs rob adolescents of precious time, stamina, and health. They interrupt critical learning processes, sometimes forever. Teenagers who use drugs are likely to withdraw increasingly into themselves, to "cop out" at just the time when they most need to reach out and experience the world.

Adolescence is a time of change, both physical and emotional, both scary and exciting. Educating teenagers about their changing bodies and feelings often makes the process much less frightening for them.

Fortunately, as a recent Gallup poll shows, young people are beginning to realize this, too. They themselves label drugs their most important problem. In the last few years, moreover, the climate of tolerance and ignorance surrounding drugs has been changing.

Adolescents as well as adults are becoming aware of mounting evidence that every race, ethnic group, and class is vulnerable to drug dependency.

Recent publicity about the cost and failure of drug rehabilitation efforts; dangerous drug use among pilots, air traffic controllers, star athletes, and Hollywood celebrities; and drug-related accidents, suicides, and violent crime have focused the public's attention on the need to wage an all-out war on drug abuse before it seriously undermines the fabric of society itself.

The anti-drug message is getting stronger and there is evidence that the message is beginning to get through to adults and teenagers alike.

FOREWORD

The Encyclopedia of Psychoactive Drugs hopes to play a part in the national campaign now underway to educate young people about drugs. Series 1 provides clear and comprehensive discussions of common psychoactive substances, outlines their psychological and physiological effects on the mind and body, explains how they "hook" the user, and separates fact from myth in the complex issue of drug abuse.

Whereas Series 1 focuses on specific drugs, such as nicotine or cocaine, Series 2 confronts a broad range of both social and physiological phenomena. Each volume addresses the ramifications of drug use and abuse on some aspect of human experience: social, familial, cultural, historical, and physical. Separate volumes explore questions about the effects of drugs on brain chemistry and unborn children; the use and abuse of painkillers; the relationship between drugs and sexual behavior, sports, and the arts; drugs and disease; the role of drugs in history; and the sophisticated drugs now being developed in the laboratory that will profoundly change the future.

Each book in the series is fully illustrated and is tailored to the needs and interests of young readers. The more adolescents know about drugs and their role in society, the less likely they are to misuse them.

Joann Rodgers
Senior Editorial Consultant

An early-20th-century depiction of a seduction. From the brain's standpoint, sexuality is the only concept that is driven entirely by pleasure — a feeling that does not have to be enhanced by drugs.

INTRODUCTION

The Gift of Wizardry Use and Abuse

JACK H. MENDELSON, M.D.
NANCY K. MELLO, Ph.D.
*Alcohol and Drug Abuse Research Center
Harvard Medical School—McLean Hospital*

Dorothy to the Wizard:
"I think you are a very bad man," said Dorothy.
"Oh no, my dear; I'm really a very good man; but I'm a very bad Wizard."
—from THE WIZARD OF OZ

Man is endowed with the gift of wizardry, a talent for discovery and invention. The discovery and invention of substances that change the way we feel and behave are among man's special accomplishments, and, like so many other products of our wizardry, these substances have the capacity to harm as well as to help. Psychoactive drugs can cause profound changes in the chemistry of the brain and other vital organs, and although their legitimate use can relieve pain and cure disease, their abuse leads in a tragic number of cases to destruction.

Consider alcohol — available to all and yet regarded with intense ambivalence from biblical times to the present day. The use of alcoholic beverages dates back to our earliest ancestors. Alcohol use and misuse became associated with the worship of gods and demons. One of the most powerful Greek gods was Dionysus, lord of fruitfulness and god of wine. The Romans adopted Dionysus but changed his name to Bacchus. Festivals and holidays associated with Bacchus celebrated the harvest and the origins of life. Time has blurred the images of the Bacchanalian festival, but the theme of drunkenness as a major part of celebration has survived the pagan gods and remains a familiar part of modern society. The term "Bacchanalian Festival" conveys a more appealing image than "drunken orgy" or "pot party," but whatever the label, drinking alcohol is a form of drug use that results in addiction for millions.

The fact that many millions of other people can use alcohol in moderation does not mitigate the toll this drug takes on society as a whole. According to reliable estimates, one out of every ten Americans develops a serious alcohol-related problem sometime in his or her lifetime. In addition, automobile accidents caused by drunken drivers claim the lives of tens of thousands every year. Many of the victims are gifted young people, just starting out in adult life. Hospital emergency rooms abound with patients seeking help for alcohol-related injuries.

Who is to blame? Can we blame the many manufacturers who produce such an amazing variety of alcoholic beverages? Should we blame the educators who fail to explain the perils of intoxication, or so exaggerate the dangers of drinking that no one could possibly believe them? Are friends to blame — those peers who urge others to "drink more and faster," or the macho types who stress the importance of being able to "hold your liquor"? Casting blame, however, is hardly constructive, and pointing the finger is a fruitless way to deal with the problem. Alcoholism and drug abuse have few culprits but many victims. Accountability begins with each of us, every time we choose to use or misuse an intoxicating substance.

It is ironic that some of man's earliest medicines, derived from natural plant products, are used today to poison and to intoxicate. Relief from pain and suffering is one of society's many continuing goals. Over 3,000 years ago, the Therapeutic Papyrus of Thebes, one of our earliest written records, gave instructions for the use of opium in the treatment of pain. Opium, in the form of its major derivative, morphine, and similar compounds, such as heroin, have also been used by many to induce changes in mood and feeling. Another example of man's misuse of a natural substance is the coca leaf, which for centuries was used by the Indians of Peru to reduce fatigue and hunger. Its modern derivative, cocaine, has important medical use as a local anesthetic. Unfortunately, its

INTRODUCTION

increasing abuse in the 1980s clearly has reached epidemic proportions.

The purpose of this series is to explore in depth the psychological and behavioral effects that psychoactive drugs have on the individual, and also, to investigate the ways in which drug use influences the legal, economic, cultural, and even moral aspects of societies. The information presented here (and in other books in this series) is based on many clinical and laboratory studies and other observations by people from diverse walks of life.

Over the centuries, novelists, poets, and dramatists have provided us with many insights into the sometimes seductive but ultimately problematic aspects of alcohol and drug use. Physicians, lawyers, biologists, psychologists, and social scientists have contributed to a better understanding of the causes and consequences of using these substances. The authors in this series have attempted to gather and condense all the latest information about drug use and abuse. They have also described the sometimes wide gaps in our knowledge and have suggested some new ways to answer many difficult questions.

One such question, for example, is how do alcohol and drug problems get started? And what is the best way to treat them when they do? Not too many years ago, alcoholics and drug abusers were regarded as evil, immoral, or both. It is now recognized that these persons suffer from very complicated diseases involving deep psychological and social problems. To understand how the disease begins and progresses, it is necessary to understand the nature of the substance, the behavior of addicts, and the characteristics of the society or culture in which they live.

Although many of the social environments we live in are very similar, some of the most subtle differences can strongly influence our thinking and behavior. Where we live, go to school and work, whom we discuss things with — all influence our opinions about drug use and misuse. Yet we also share certain commonly accepted beliefs that outweigh any differences in our attitudes. The authors in this series have tried to identify and discuss the central, most crucial issues concerning drug use and misuse.

Despite the increasing sophistication of the chemical substances we create in the laboratory, we have a long way to go in our efforts to make these powerful drugs work for us rather than against us.

The volumes in this series address a wide range of timely questions. What influence has drug use had on the arts? Why do so many of today's celebrities and star athletes use drugs, and what is being done to solve this problem? What is the relationship between drugs and crime? What is the physiological basis for the power drugs can hold over us? These are but a few of the issues explored in this far-ranging series.

Educating people about the dangers of drugs can go a long way towards minimizing the desperate consequences of substance abuse for individuals and society as a whole. Luckily, human beings have the resources to solve even the most serious problems that beset them, once they make the commitment to do so. As one keen and sensitive observer, Dr. Lewis Thomas, has said,

> There is nothing at all absurd about the human condition. We matter. It seems to me a good guess, hazarded by a good many people who have thought about it, that we may be engaged in the formation of something like a mind for the life of this planet. If this is so, we are still at the most primitive stage, still fumbling with language and thinking, but infinitely capacitated for the future. Looked at this way, it is remarkable that we've come as far as we have in so short a period, really no time at all as geologists measure time. We are the newest, youngest, and the brightest thing around.

DRUGS & SEXUAL BEHAVIOR

A young couple shares a marijuana joint. Early experimentation with drugs and sexual activity often go hand in hand. This is perhaps because both have the allure of the forbidden.

AUTHOR'S PREFACE

Adolescence is a time of growth and change. It is a time of letting go of childish mannerisms and of trying on adult behavior. For many young people it can also be a time of great confusion and emotional upheaval, for in addition to the many social changes that may occur during adolescence, there are a number of physical ones as well. Puberty usually occurs between the ages of 9 and 13, though it may occur a little later in boys than in girls. During puberty the sex organs become capable of reproduction, and, at the same time, the body begins to mature in many other ways.

Unfortunately, drugs play a role in a frightening number of teenagers' search for what is new, adult, and exciting. If there is any topic among teens — and adults, too — about which more is believed and less is known than drugs, it is sex. Both subjects seem to attract misinformation at a rate approaching the speed of sound.

There is really nothing new about experimentation with drugs or sex. There is evidence, for example, that ancient cultures used a wide variety of substances, including potions, pills, and scents, to enhance sexual activity. In the 20th century, however, there are new risks to these experiments. The wide availability of "recreational" drugs such as alcohol, marijuana, and cocaine, the sexual revolution, and the danger of contracting chronic or deadly sexually transmitted diseases presents today's young people with issues and problems unimaginable in the past.

In other words, the *context* in which drugs and sexual behavior are thought about and acted on is vastly different from what it was a generation or more ago.

Recent studies estimate that the majority of adolescents have had intercourse by the time they leave high school, and more than a fourth while still in junior high. Unfortunately, peer pressure to perform sexually at very young ages comes just at a time when drugs become readily available in the adolescent's environment. Early experimentation with sexual activity often goes hand-in-hand with experimentation with drugs, perhaps because both have the allure of the forbidden.

But drugs rarely, if ever, satisfactorily enhance sex and may, in the long run, permanently impair the user's ability to function sexually at all. For those people who have sexual dysfunctions or are sexually impaired because of physical illness, however, drug therapy is available and in some cases is quite successful. The drugs used in therapy are prescribed for use in a medical setting and often improve sexual function as a side effect, not as a main benefit. Because of this, they rarely have a sexually beneficial effect on a normal, healthy person and can, in fact, be dangerous if taken without a doctor's supervision.

Much of the uneasiness young people feel about their own sexuality is usually a matter of lack of information, inexperience, embarrassment, or tension; rarely is it a matter of any psychological or physical disorder. Psychoactive drugs only cloud the issue and can, on their own, create physical problems that may interfere with sexual development.

Myths, Misconceptions, and the Media

Putting aspirin in beer makes it more intoxicating, and sipping the beer through a straw makes the drinker "uninhibited." A little marijuana guarantees sex that Hollywood would run out of *X*s trying to rate. Vitamin E makes people sexier, men more virile.

All of these statements, made by teenagers who honestly believed them, are false. Over the years, an entire mythology of misconceptions has grown up around sex and the various substances that could be used to enhance it. For example, nearly all of the ingredients of liqueurs and cordials were found to be listed among ancient Arab, Chinese, and Hindu recipes for aphrodisiacs, or "love potions" (named for the Greek goddess of love, Aphrodite). In modern society, the belief that alcohol has magical properties has diminished, but many people still feel it can be used as a tool of seduction, and that a few drinks can persuade girls to do something they may have mixed feelings about doing.

There are a number of other substances that have been mislabeled aphrodisiacs through the years and about which rumors still exist. Oysters, though they may have nutritional value, in no way enhance sex. The same holds true for olives, and that persistent but phony teen aphrodisiac, green M&Ms.

Today, rumors, usually spread by adolescents themselves, coupled with the exaggerations and distortions generated by the entertainment industry, are the modern equivalent of the myths and rituals of long ago, perpetuating many of the ancient misconceptions of sex enhancers and love potions. Popular programs repeatedly show alcohol used as a tool of seduction, relaxing the person being seduced (usually a woman) until she simply falls into her seducer's arms. Movies depict drug-induced orgies where intoxicated innocents are swept into the "glamorous" world of sex.

But the popular saying "only in the movies" holds true when it comes to the glamorization of sex and drugs. Drugs are not a safe or effective way to enhance sexual pleasure. This book will discuss the different stages of sexual arousal and the role that hormones, natural substances in the body that have druglike effects, play in those stages. It will reveal the myths surrounding different substances thought to be aphrodisiacs and explain the effects drugs can have on sexuality. It will also explore the topic of sexual dysfunction, although it is rare in teenagers, and the various drug and nondrug therapies that are being used to treat it.

If this book has a bottom-line message, or theme, it is that legal or illegal drugs are neither effective nor safe ways to try to enhance sexual pleasure. There is not a great deal of valid research, either in the past or at present, about the effects of drugs on sexual behavior. But almost all there is strongly supports the observation by the late Alfred Kinsey, the father of modern sex research, that the best, if not the only, aphrodisiac is the human mind.

Sexual arousal is not solely the result of physical attraction but is caused by a variety of pleasurable feelings, such as the enjoyable sensations of being emotionally close to another person.

CHAPTER 1

SEXUAL AROUSAL

There is much more to sexual arousal than the way our bodies feel and react. There is also the emotional interplay, the feelings of affection between people who are attracted to each other, and the pleasurable sensations of being emotionally close to another person. Unfortunately, the countless explicit scenes of sexual intercourse that can be found in literature, films, and popular music lyrics often lead many adolescents to believe that the performance of the physical act is the most important part of any sexual encounter.

In reality, there is much more to human sexuality than just sex. All humans are sexual beings from infancy. Anyone who has ever seen a baby touch his own body or cry to be held knows how true that is. But sexual feelings and experiences vary from individual to individual, and what is right for one person may not be right for another. Different people choose different ways to express their sexuality. In her book *Changing Bodies, Changing Lives*, author Ruth Bell defines true sexuality in this way:

> Being sexual can mean having sexy thoughts or feelings, loving to be touched, enjoying the way other people's bodies look, touching your body in places that feel particularly good, making up romantic or sexy stories in your head that you might or might not ever act out, kissing and touching someone you feel attracted to.... Sexuality is much fuller and more varied than just lovemaking.... Our bodies are alive to sexual feelings.

Sensuality, including the desire to be held and hugged, is inherent in the human psyche and manifests itself in earliest childhood.

What all this sexual behavior means is that nature makes it very easy for normal human beings to become sexually aroused and sexually fulfilled — without drugs. It means that there is immense variety in the ways by which sexual arousal and pleasure occur. To understand more fully why this is so, it helps to understand the physiology, or process of sexual arousal and sexual response.

Understanding the Physical Response

Perhaps the most well-known of all studies of sexual behavior took place during the 1960s, under the direction of Dr. William Masters and Virginia Johnson. Masters and Johnson revealed that the physical response of your body to sexual excitement generally follows a cycle that begins with a gradual increase in emotional and physical excitement, intensifies during a plateau period, climaxes with an orgasm, and ends with a return to a relaxed state. It is necessary, however, to note several important things about this cycle.

First, no one completes every phase of the cycle every time. In fact, it is quite common for young adults to stop at the excitement stage, preferring to abstain from the more advanced stages of sexual activity until they are both physically and emotionally equipped to handle them.

Second, contrary to popular belief, essentially the same process occurs in both boys and girls, although some stages of the process are more visible in boys than in girls.

Third, there is no right or wrong way to begin, go through, or end the sexual response cycle. Arousal, plateau, climax, and relaxation can and do occur during masturbation, dreams, petting, and intercourse. Experts tell us, for example, that arousal and even orgasm occur in response to erotic thoughts, fantasies, or images processed solely by the brain, without any physical contact or stimulation at all. The same responses occur with genital sex, oral sex, kissing, and massage. Moreover, some people never have orgasms, or have very few, but still enjoy their sexuality.

William Masters and Virginia Johnson, who during the 1960s conducted a pioneering study of sexual behavior. Their work revealed that sexual response generally follows a four-part cycle.

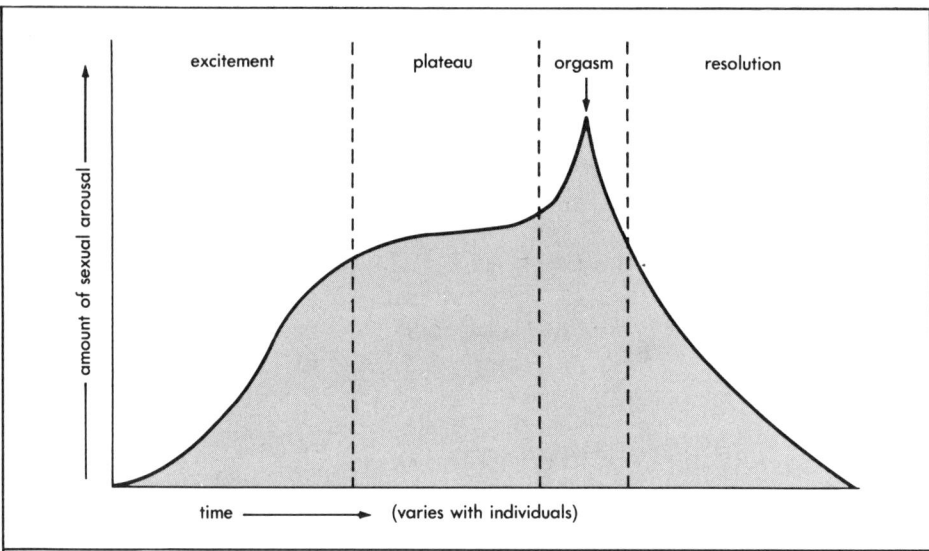

Figure 1: The Sexual Response Cycle. Although there are four phases in the sexual response cycle, not everyone experiences all four during every sexual encounter.

Fourth, it is true that boys tend to have orgasms more easily than girls. Simple anatomy is one reason. Boys figure out very early in life how to trigger an orgasm by masturbating. A girl's principal organ of sexual pleasure, the clitoris, is a tiny knob of tissue located above the opening of the vagina in the female vulva. Because the clitoris is not easily reached and difficult to see, learning how to initiate an orgasm is a bit more complicated for girls.

Fifth, although sexual arousal and response are essentially the same for both sexes, there are some physical differences. In girls, for example, there is more vasocongestion, or swelling, of the skin over the body during sexual arousal than in boys. The swelling and congested feeling that accompanies sexual arousal is much more specialized and complicated in boys than in girls, but is also easily lost. Females are rarely impotent, or incapable of sexual arousal, and they are able to become and stay aroused more often and for longer periods of time than males. On the other hand, girls often have more difficulty reaching orgasm than do boys.

Finally, there are also cultural and emotional differences between male and female sexuality. "In general," says sex therapist Dr. Helen Singer Kaplan, "it appears that the female sexual response is more variable than a male's, presumably because it is far more susceptible to psychological and cultural determinants. In contrast, sexual arousal in the male, especially when he is young, is governed to a greater extent by physical factors and is less vulnerable, although by no means immune to [psychological] influences."

The Sexual Response Cycle

It should be noted that there is no distinct beginning and end of any of the four stages of sexual arousal, and that one often follows the other without the individual being aware of the progression.

Excitement, the first phase in the cycle, is often caused by feelings of both physical and emotional closeness. During this period, blood rushes to the three areas of spongy tissue located in the boy's penis, causing it to become erect. There is increased lubrication in the girl's vagina, which increases in width and length, and the clitoris swells and becomes erect. There is also an enlargement of the womb, which lifts up slightly from its usual resting place on the floor of the pelvis, lending a further feeling of congestion.

Both the male and female nipples become hard and erect, and there is often a reddening over the upper torso, referred to as the "sex flush." There is also a marked increase in muscular tension, heart beat, and blood pressure.

The *plateau*, the second phase of the sexual response cycle, occurs as a result of continued stimulation. In boys, the testicles become so filled with blood they are 50% larger than normal, and the head of the penis becomes even more swollen. In girls, the "lips" of the vagina balloon in shape and become almost purple in color; the clitoris, too sensitive for direct stimulation at this stage, pulls in under a hood of skin.

If the sex flush has not appeared in an earlier stage, it usually does so now. There is a further increase in heart rate, muscular tension, and blood pressure. Breathing becomes shallow and rapid.

The next stage, *orgasm*, or *climax*, involves a release in the muscular tension that has built up in the previous stages. This normally involves a series of pleasurable muscle spasms that lasts approximately 10 seconds. Climax can be enor-

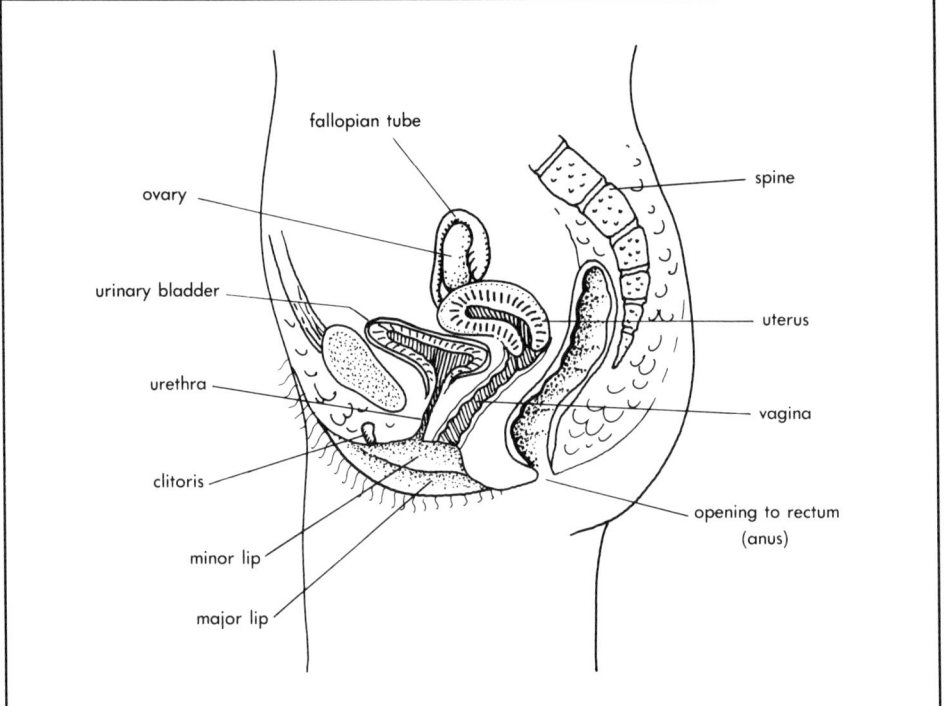

The Female Reproductive System. *During puberty the reproductive organs mature; the ovaries begin releasing eggs, signifying that the woman is now capable of reproduction.*

mously powerful, involving strong shudders felt throughout the body. At other times, it is a spreading warmth, almost relaxing and peaceful. In the male, muscles in the ejaculatory duct push the semen out of the penis — either a few drops at a time or in a sudden surge. This is known as ejaculation. Scientists now also believe that women experience something very similar to male ejaculation, though it is not neccesarily as easily apparent.

During *resolution* or *relaxation*, the final stage, the body begins its return to the normal, unaroused state. The muscles become relaxed, and heart rate, breathing, and blood pressure return to normal. The nipples lose their hardness, the sex flush disappears, and the penis rapidly shrinks down to its normal, unaroused size.

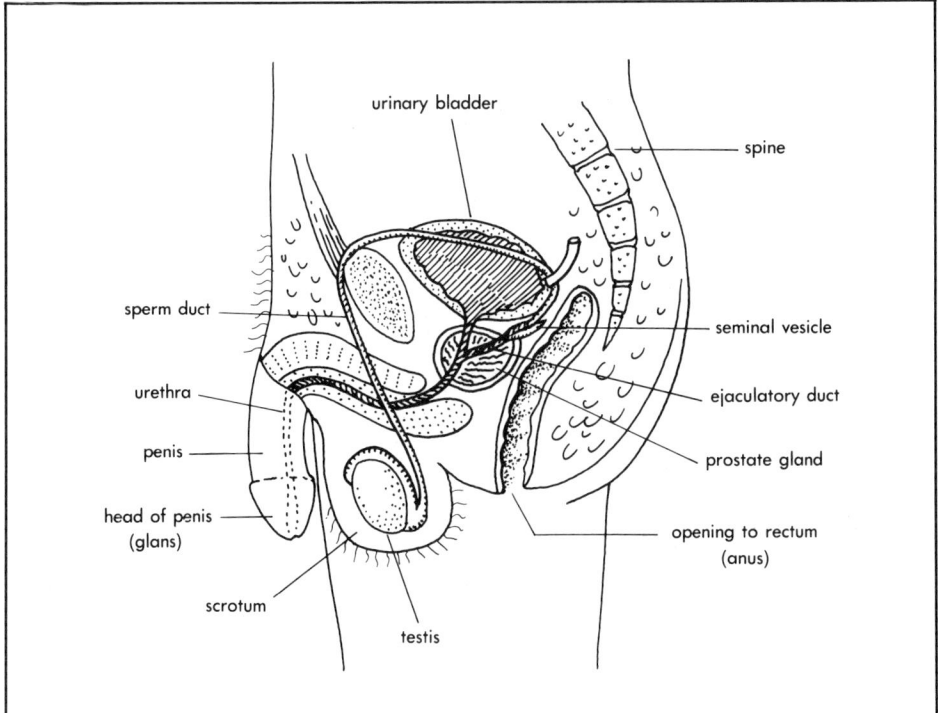

The Male Reproductive System. *Psychoactive drugs often interfere with a man's ability to become aroused. He may also be unable to sustain an erection or to ejaculate.*

After orgasm, the male enters a *refractory period*, during which he is unable to reach orgasm. Refractory periods can last anywhere from a few minutes to a few days, depending upon age and sexual stimulation and needs. Females do not have refractory periods and can often remain stimulated and capable of orgasm during the resolution period.

Sex, Instinct, and Learning

When animals mate, neither the male nor the female needs to be wined or dined or romanced. The purpose is to reproduce, thus assuring the survival of the species. Neither gender looks for the animal world's equivalent of a highball, or love drug, or checks an X-rated movie out of the local video club to help "get in the mood."

The sexual drive in animals, unlike that in humans, is strictly instinctual and is designed exclusively for the purpose of reproducing and ensuring the survival of the species.

This is because in animals the sex drive is a tool of survival, programmed by nature. In most mammals, for example, sexual arousal is closely linked to chemical substances called *pheromones*, which the female releases when she is in heat, or fertile. Pheromones signal to the males of the species that a particular female is in heat and ready to be mated with.

There is no scientific evidence, however, that humans, like other mammals, are attracted by sexual smells. With humans, the physiology of sexual attraction between sexes is far more subtle and only partly dependent on chemical cues. It differs from that of other mammals in that sexual activity is not restricted to those times of the month when a woman can conceive a child, and human males are not driven to mate by the presence of pheromones. With humans, sex is pleasurable in and of itself and is sought whether or not a child is wanted.

In other mammals, the erotic triggers are very specific and always the same for a particular species. A male chimpanzee, for instance, will not mate unless a female is in heat, displays her body in a certain way, and gives off a particular smell.

Studies in which such females are "deodorized" show that the male will simply not respond. Similarly, when the females and males are stopped from making certain movements, postures, and physical contacts, their interest in sex stops instantly.

In humans, we know that this is not the case. Human sexuality and sexual behavior are truly *psychosomatic* (governed by the mind and the emotions), with the psychological aspects dominating the biological. To be sure, purely biological (or hormonal) factors play a role in sexual response. However, what people learn, and the influence of their family, society, religion, education, and memory play at least as large a role, and in many cases, override purely physical factors.

As Johns Hopkins sexual researcher Dr. John Money notes, hormones are essential, but so is "the dominance of ... learned factors in the overt expression of eroticism in man. Erotic arousal may be generated by signals to the brain for the eyes, ears and sense of smell, [and be] erotically just as potent as [those from the sex organs]."

The precise role hormones play in human sexuality is unclear. It is known, however, that they are involved in the development of the sex organs and play a role in regulating the sex drive.

CHAPTER 2

HORMONES: NATURE'S OWN DRUGS

Sex and hormones are closely allied in our minds. We talk about "raging hormones" among teenagers in love and unable to think of little else but sexual encounters. We read of rapists who are treated with hormones to lower their sex drives. Most of what we learn in textbooks about puberty focuses on testosterone, estrogen, and the other sex hormones.

The links between hormones and sexuality are quite real. Sex hormones concentrate selectively in certain parts of the brain, among them the hypothalamus, a glandlike organ that automatically regulates and monitors sex drive, body temperature, hunger, the menstrual cycle, some emotions, and the hormones secreted by the pituitary gland, a small rounded structure at the base of the brain. Hormones also play a role in the development of sex organs.

Thanks to the work of thousands of scientists, including psychiatrists, psychologists, endocrinologists (hormone specialists), anatomists, and specialists in prenatal development, we now know a good deal about our sexual chemistry. But even though many facts are known, the role of hormones remains too often misunderstood and misrepresented.

In this chapter, we will begin to put the role of sex hormones and other sexual chemicals in perspective, providing details about where they come from, what influences them, and how they are regulated.

The passage from childhood to adulthood involves learning what it means to be a sexual being. Some experts believe that teenage drug abuse delays or halts the development of adult sexuality.

A knowledge of our hormonal chemistry can do three things: raise sensitivity to the complicated chemical loops involved in sexual response; highlight the absurdity of claims made for various and sundry "love drugs"; and provide a warning about the dangers of interfering in the fragile balance of our biochemical scales.

To begin to understand sex hormones, it is necessary first to look at the activity of the brain in human sexuality. At its most basic level, the sex drive is controlled by the brain, specifically the hypothalamus, located deep at the back of the brain.

Scientists investigating the connections between brain and behavior had for a long time suspected the existence of a close tie between areas of the brain that regulated sexual behavior and the pleasure centers of the brain. In recent years, those suspicions have been confirmed by tracking the interactions between the hypothalamus and other brain areas.

The hypothalamus is the link between our endocrine system, or glands — which produce hormones — and the nervous system. Hypothalamic activities are closely connected to activities regulated by the limbic system, a wishbone-shaped structure that wraps around the top of the brainstem. The limbic system controls emotions and mood.

The close links among specific areas of the brain, brain chemicals, and feelings of well-being, pleasure, and sex evolved to assure survival of the human species. Also for survival's sake, all levels of the brain are involved at some point in sexual activity, sending and receiving signals from the sex organs and nerve cells and regulating sexual reflexes that are influenced by everything from fear and hate to love and fantasy.

Studies in primates (a class of mammals including monkeys, apes, and man) show that impulses activated by sexual arousal and orgasm are relayed via electrical impulses and brain chemicals to the pleasure centers, reinforcing in the strongest possible way the desire for sex. Moreover, certain brain areas that are involved in arousal are linked to areas that produce pleasure when stimulated during experiments.

From the brain's standpoint, sexuality is the only activity that is driven entirely by pleasure; experiments show that only direct electrical (or chemical) stimulation of the pleasure zones in the limbic system come close, in the words of sex expert Dr. Helen Singer Kaplan, to "rivaling the intense pleasure of eros or of producing cravings as intense as sexual ones."

Sex hormones interact with brain, anatomical, and physical activities. In the female, sex hormones are manufactured principally in the ovaries, the pair of almond-shaped organs in the female pelvic area that produce and release eggs. In the male, sex hormones are manufactured principally in the testes, the pair of male sex glands contained in the scrotal sac outside the torso that also make and release sperm.

•Androgens. The word *androgen* is taken from the Greek word for man. Androgens are principally male sex hormones. The main androgen is testosterone, which promotes and controls the development of male sex organs and the "secondary" sex characteristics we associate with men, such as facial hair and a deep voice.

But thanks to the work of Drs. John Money and Anke Ehrhardt, among others, we know that androgens, present at the moment of conception, exert important influences on the development of unborn babies of *both* sexes and on their later sexual behavior.

In boys, at puberty, the hypothalamus directs the pituitary gland at the base of the brain to increase the output of LH (luteinizing hormone), FSH (follicle-stimulating hormone), and other hormones actually found in both sexes in varying amounts. These act on the testes and adrenal glands located near the kidney to start increased production of testosterone.

Evidence suggests that boys exposed to too-low ratios of androgen to female hormones before birth may be somewhat "feminized" and that females exposed to too-high ratios of androgens may be somewhat "masculinized."

In adults, sex drive and potency can be profoundly reduced if testosterone levels become depleted. Androgens, which trigger sexual-interest centers in the brains of both sexes, are necessary for a healthy sex drive in women as well as men. Some studies suggest that women deprived of sources of androgen (removal of their ovaries or adrenal glands) may entirely lose their interest in sex.

Like all sex hormones, androgens increase and decrease in number at various rates. And these rates depend greatly on psychological and social factors. Depression, for example, can markedly lower testosterone levels. Falling in love can, on the other hand, bring the most satisfying sexual experiences even when androgen levels are low.

- Estrogens. Estrogens are the principal female sex hormones. At puberty, the ovaries begin to secrete large amounts of estrogen and progesterone, which start and control menstruation. Also at the onset of puberty, LH and FSH stimulate the ovaries and adrenal glands to secrete androgens that widen women's hips and trigger the development of breasts and pubic hair.

- Progesterone. Progesterone is a steroid hormone (sex hormone released by the adrenal cortex) responsible for the changes in the uterus during the second half of the menstrual cycle, development of the maternal placenta (the spongy structure in the pregnant woman's uterus from which the fetus derives nourishment) after the implantation of the egg during conception, and the development of the mammary glands in women's breasts.

Unlike androgens, estrogen and progesterone do not appear to have any potent influence on sexual behavior, although a reduction in them may in fact *increase* the female sex drive by giving androgens that are present more opportunity to influence body and brain.

All levels of the brain are involved at some point in sexual activity, including attraction, arousal, and response.

Studies by Masters and Johnson in recent years suggest that for many women, sexual arousal and intense orgasms are more likely to occur just before, during, and just after menstruation, when estrogen and progesterone levels are at their lowest. Other researchers, however, have found that erotic interest is highest when estrogen levels are highest — at midcycle.

The picture is at best cloudy with respect to the role of female sex hormones and sexual desire. Women, it seems, are far more able than men to experience sexual interest independently of their hormones.

We know that if supplies of testosterone, the principal male sex hormone, are cut off, sex drive is reduced or even stopped altogether in males; and, if a man — or a woman — takes testosterone under certain conditions, the hormone will strengthen the sex drive.

Adolescence is a time of emotional volatility. This is partly because the enormous hormonal changes that occur during the teenage years can have a profound influence on mood.

As early as 1961 psychologists found that women who for medical reasons took androgen supplements ("masculinizing" hormones found in both males and females) could expect a genuine increase in sexual interest. This increase in sexual interest was so marked that one observer called the results "unladylike."

The use of estrogen to fend off the worst effects of menopause in women and the use of certain brain hormones whose loss is linked to aging have also worked with some individuals as "rejuvenators" of sexual drive and performance.

Unfortunately, despite occasional success with the use of hormones as aphrodisiacs, balanced scientific studies demonstrate clearly that attempts to use hormones to initiate, enhance, or strengthen sexual interest and action generally work only when the chemicals replace abnormally missing natural supplies, not when they are added to normal hormone supplies.

Sex Hormones and Sexual Behavior

If anyone doubts the largely insignificant role of sex hormones on sexual behavior, consider the dramatic studies of hermaphrodites. Hermaphrodites are people who, because of abnormal prenatal development, are born with the sexual organs and hormone potential of both sexes, male and female. Decades-long follow-up studies of such children show that they will grow up feeling and behaving like whatever sex they were assigned and reared to be, regardless of what hormones are circulating or not circulating in their bodies. When parents and physicians agreed a child would be treated, dressed, and cared for as a girl and such a child underwent surgery to make appearances consistent with female anatomy, the child functioned as a girl and, subsequently, as a woman in every way. If the decision was made to raise a boy, a similar outcome occurred.

What, then, can we conclude about the role of sex hormones and their possible role as aphrodisiacs?

Many experts believe that for both men and women, perhaps the only true "love hormone" is androgen. Men given estrogens for the treatment of certain diseases, for example, report decreased sex drive. Women given androgens for cancer therapy report increased sexual desire. Men who suffered

Many experts, such as the sex researcher John Money, believe that excessive supplies of hormones will not enhance a person's sex life and may, in fact, be a hazard to his or her health.

from a decrease in androgen levels, related to advanced age or illness, experienced a marked decrease in sexual desire and performance. Estrogen therapy for women after menopause has been reported to increase interest in sex, but most likely because the hormones increase blood supply to the genital tract.

However, experts also find that the androgen connection is highly complex, with "irregularities that cannot be explained," in one scientist's words. At best, androgens' role as aphrodisiacs is inconsistent and unpredictable, except in cases where normal supplies are completely cut off as a result of injury, birth defects, or serious illness.

The record, based on experiments and sexual therapy cases, suggests that nature's supply and use of hormones is carefully balanced and influenced by both physical and psychological health. In people whose supplies are excessive, the result is not "better sex," but ill health, and the use of sex hormones in healthy people to stimulate better sex would seem to be, in many ways, unnatural.

Dr. John Money, like many experts on the subject of human sexuality, goes so far as to say that "the sex hormones ... have no direct effect on the direction or content or erotic inclinations in the human species."

The belief that certain substances can arouse sexual desire is as old as civilization itself. But the truth is that oysters, which vaguely resemble female sex organs, and wine, which lowers inhibitions, do not have the aphrodisiac powers legend has attributed to them.

CHAPTER 3

APHRODISIACS: FACT OR FICTION?

Derived from the Greek word for love or desire, an aphrodisiac is a substance that, once ingested, can arouse sexual desire — often in an unsuspecting or reluctant partner. The belief that certain substances are aphrodisiacs is as old as civilization itself. Certain substances were thought to have special powers because they resembled sexual organs. Oysters, eggs, onions, and clams, because they were in shapes that suggested the female sex organs, became popular. Pulverized rhinoceros horn, bananas, deer antlers, sausages, asparagus, and celery stalks, with their resemblance to the male sex organ, were also ingested.

Raven gall, sesame oil, pumpkin seeds, gold, silver, and lead shavings also enjoyed a brief vogue, though the reasons why are lost to the past. Although the use of these substances may seem incredible to us now, the 20th century has some remarkable, if quite untrue, beliefs of its own. The search for and belief in the existence of aphrodisiacs are still evident today, and a wide variety of substances, some dangerous, are believed to have powers of sexual persuasion.

DRUGS AND SEXUAL BEHAVIOR

Aphrodisiacs are named for Aphrodite, the Greek goddess of love, beauty, and fertility. According to mythology Aphrodite was the epitome of womanly beauty and was adored by gods and mortals alike.

• Cantharides (Spanish Fly). This is, perhaps, the best known of all alleged aphrodisiacs, and rumors and stories detailing the powers of Spanish Fly abound. Made from the outer coating of a small beetle, this drug irritates sensitive body membranes, causing them to itch. One theory holds that Spanish Fly causes an itch inside a woman's vagina, and because of this, she will crave sexual intercourse to "scratch" it. In men, cantharides causes a large, but painful, erection.

The drug is considered a poison and is available only in underground drug stores or on the street. Furthermore, it has been known to cause both lethal convulsions and kidney failure in its users.

• Yohimbine. Made for the most part from a large double-trunked African tree, yohimbine was considered an aphrodisiac long ago because of the tree's faintly humanoid shape. An alkaloid substance chemically related to LSD, yohimbine has been mixed with male sex hormones and strychnine to treat impotence in older men. However, because the drug adversely affects the heart and can, even in relatively small doses, cause panic attacks, it is no longer available for medical purposes. Its reputation as an aphrodisiac probably arose because, in the brain, it causes the release of greater levels of norepinephrine, a neurotransmitter that regulates sexual activity.

•Ginseng. Ginseng is a plant that was once believed to be an aphrodisiac because its forked root resembles a human being with limbs. However, it has no mind- or body-altering properties. Its only value is that it contains some vitamins.

•Nutmeg (*Myristica fragrans*). A spice native to Indonesia, nutmeg is related to a group of chemicals somewhat similar in structure to amphetamines. A drug user must consume large amounts of nutmeg to experience its psychoactive effects. The consumption of nutmeg causes unpleasant symptoms, such as red eyes, nausea, headache, agitation, hyperactivity, sleeplessness, dry mouth and throat, and motor and speech difficulties. After several hours the drug user may experience euphoria and visual hallucinations. However, it may take several days for the feeling of nausea to pass. During this period the user sometimes suffers from depression, tiredness, and aching bones and muscles. In doses high enough to cause hallucinations, nutmeg causes a complete loss of interest in sex, and the user usually becomes ill.

•Strychnine. Extracted from the plant *nux vomica*, strychnine has been reported to sustain sexual arousal. Unfortunately, it is also a deadly poison, used most often for killing rodents.

•Alcohol. As Shakespeare wrote in *Macbeth*, "It provokes the desire, but it takes away the performance." In small to moderate amounts, alcohol first gives the impression of being a stimulant. "There's a nice, warm jolt," was how one 15 year old described it. "You feel just a little high. I feel sexier and I'm not so shy around the guys."

In reality, alcohol produces its effects by depressing the central nervous system. In a study by Dr. Sharon C. Wilsnack of the Harvard Medical School, women said that alcohol initially made them feel "warm, loving, considerate, expressive, open, affectionate, sexy and feminine," whereas men mostly reported feeling a sense of power.

For a short time, those who have either one mixed drink or two glasses of beer or wine over an hour's time may feel freer about sex, more willing to participate, less anxious, less attentive to rules, values, and their usual good judgment. But taken in larger amounts, alcohol's depressant actions make having satisfying sex more difficult, if not impossible, especially for males. Once the uninhibited couple gets to bed, the alcohol may have made them drowsy and relatively clumsy. The sensory pleasures of touch are numbed. Getting and keeping an erection may become problematic. Alcohol slows the firing of nerves and the movement of muscles that serve the genitals and other parts of the body. Thus, arousal and climax are delayed or precluded.

Although many women have said that drinking alcohol makes them feel more "sexy and feminine," the drug does not enhance — and can preclude — sexual enjoyment for people of both sexes.

APHRODISIACS: FACT OR FICTION?

Numerous studies have proven that alcohol alters sex hormone levels, numbs sensory pleasure, and interferes with muscle movement. These actions increase the risk of impotence in men.

Although no one knows precisely how alcohol works on the brain, the most widely accepted theory is that it suppresses the "higher level" centers that keep our conscious behavior under control, long before it interferes with speech, muscle control, and more obvious behaviors.

Numerous studies provide evidence that alcohol can alter sex hormone levels, increase the risk of impotence in men, and decrease sexual arousal in women. Several experiments show decreased testosterone levels in the blood of men who drink. In one study of 17,000 alcoholic men, 8% had bouts of impotence they admitted to; in half of these cases, the impotence was permanent.

In a study of 16 women, researchers gave them alcohol and showed them erotic movies while simultaneously using sophisticated monitors to measure vaginal congestion, one major sign of sexual arousal or "readiness" in women. In all the women, the alcohol increased the women's feelings of sexiness but in reality decreased objective signs of arousal — the vaginal congestion. Finally, in a study of 44 alcoholic women, 20% said they never experienced orgasms, whereas 36% had experienced them less than 5% of the time.

The average drinker, however, often does not realize that there is anything wrong with his or her behavior or body. In fact, he or she may feel quite the contrary. This is because in low doses — one drink or fewer per hour — alcohol has what Dr. John Money calls a "halo" effect with respect to erotic behavior. That is, alcohol can add to or enhance sexual activity when the setting for that activity raises the expectation that the alcohol will in fact do so. In larger doses, the effect is lost.

Like so many other drugs touted as aphrodisiacs, alcohol's effects depend on the person taking it and the context in which it is taken. As one physician and author notes:

> At a party [alcohol's] effects tend to give us a feeling of ... friendliness. The pretty girl seems more desirable, other people's anecdotes seem funnier and one's own flow freely. Yet the same quantity of alcohol taken alone by an unhappy, depressed individual will not lift his mood; it is more likely to remove his controls so that he weeps helplessly. Taken at bedtime, such a dose will simply make a person sleepy. Taken during a jealous quarrel, it may make one extremely aggressive. And even though the partygoer *feels* confident and therefore efficient, he is actually much less so than before. His increased sexual desire does not lead to a better sexual performance, his easy flow of conversation will be less intelligent than it is when he is sober.

"Insofar as sex is concerned," agrees Dr. Mary Calderone in *The Family Book About Sexuality*, "it is not possible to separate the actual physical effects of ... alcohol from the psychological effects. If a person thinks that a drink or a drug will make sex better for him or her, then quite possibly it will seem to do so, in spite of the fact that for others the capacity to perform may actually be lowered."

Unfortunately, the popular view of alcohol and sex as found in movies, television, and popular literature often reinforces the belief that it is a social and sexual lubricant. In fact, when consumed in excess by teenagers with limited experience, rapid physical development, and see-sawing psychological responses, alcohol may be a sexual saboteur and can lead to troubling consequences.

Although many users boast that marijuana increases sexual desire and improves performance, the drug can have a negative effect not only on the sexual act itself but also on fertility and reproduction.

CHAPTER 4

PSYCHOACTIVE DRUGS AND SEX

Perhaps the most dangerous turn in the search for aphrodisiacs has been toward the use of psychoactive drugs — many of them illicit. Taken in small doses, some drugs *can* produce pleasurable results, but the risks that are taken, and the price that is often paid, are rarely, if ever, worth the chance. For it is a matter of fact that illicit drugs can undermine sexual responsiveness, cloud judgment, and, in some cases, permanently impair the user's ability to perform sexually.

The following is a list of the most commonly used psychoactive drugs and their effects on sexual behavior. Keep in mind that little legitimate research exists on this subject as of yet and that the few effects that are known are variable at best and completely unpredictable.

•Marijuana. Though many users may boast that this drug increases sexual desire and improves performance, marijuana has been shown to have a significantly negative effect on performance and possibly on fertility and reproduction. Some users claim that marijuana can prolong orgasm and intensify muscle contractions. Research on long-term use of hashish (a more potent form of marijuana) in India, however, suggests that very large doses of the drug can decrease sexual desire and interfere with a man's ability to get an erection. Similar studies suggest that THC (the active ingredient in marijuana) decreases circulating levels of testosterone, the principal male sex hormone.

Frequent marijuana use can reduce the number and quality of sperm in a man's body, damaging their ability to move freely and thus impairing the man's fertility. Furthermore, heavy marijuana use can interfere with the working of the endocrine system, which controls hormones and metabolism. Because of this, men who smoked nine or more marijuana cigarettes a day showed a decrease in the levels of testosterone, the male hormone. Women were shown to have disrupted menstrual cycles, with the failure to ovulate normally resulting in unpredictable periods of fertility.

Heavy marijuana use can also cause breakage of and other damage to the chromosomes (the material that translates genetic information). These birth defects can appear in the offspring of the marijuana user or can skip a generation and appear later on. The continued use of marijuana during pregnancy can result in nervous system abnormalities, low birth weight, and fetal death.

•Cocaine. Cocaine is a central nervous system stimulant that can, in small doses, initially increase sexual desire and performance. This may be largely because stimulants boost activity in the brain, enabling users to stay awake and alert for longer periods of time. Stimulants also prompt the release

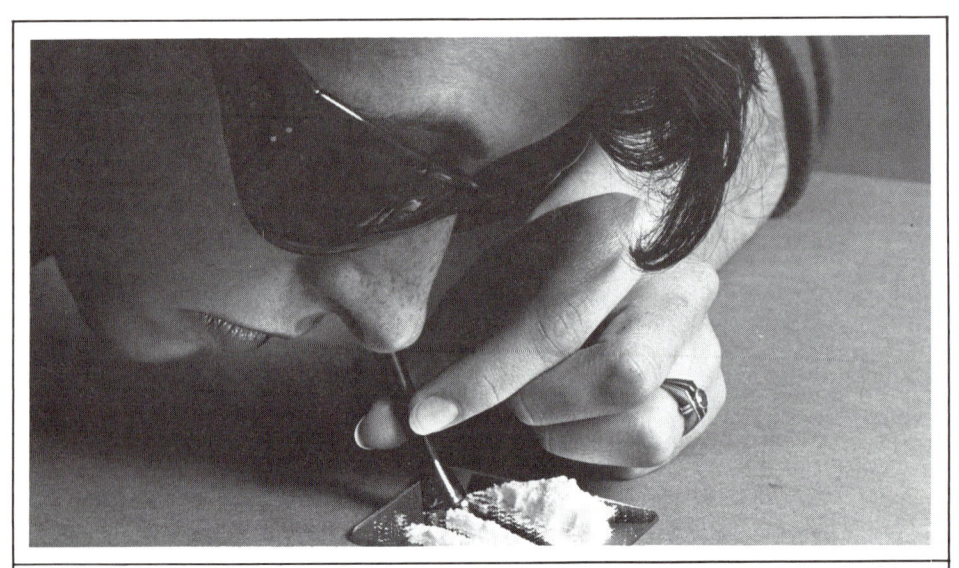

A young woman snorts cocaine. The negative side effects of this highly addictive drug far outweigh its powers as a sexual stimulant.

of the neurotransmitter (chemical messenger) norepinephrine, which directly stimulates the genitals and increases their sensitivity.

Cocaine also enhances the activity of another neurotransmitter, dopamine, which is known to help regulate the heart, blood pressure, and muscles. One theory suggests that when there is an increase in the dopamine level in the brain to the point where it exceeds the amount of serotonin, another neurotransmitter, there is a higher chance of sexual activity and responsiveness. Thus cocaine, with its side effect of increased dopamine levels in the brain, could very well be called an aphrodisiac.

Unfortunately, that is only part of the story. Cocaine also presents its own set of dangers and problems to the user. Cocaine use can cause vaginal irritations that can leave women vulnerable to injury, infection, and serious damage to their reproductive system. In long-term users, cocaine can make it difficult for men to maintain erection or to ejaculate, and for women to reach orgasm. It is also addictive and in some cases can cause heart failure and death.

- Amphetamine. Amphetamine is a stimulant, with effects very similar to those of cocaine. In fact, amphetamine and cocaine, though supposedly possessing the ability to enhance sex, both share the same list of harmful and potentially dangerous side effects. Furthermore, amphetamine can cause impotence in men; over the long term, it decreases the interest in and ability to have sex at all.

- LSD. One of the most potent hallucinogens, lysergic acid diethylamide, more commonly known as LSD, is often thought of in the context of the free sex and drug culture of the 1960s. But, in fact, little is truly known about the effects of LSD on sexual behavior. Though many LSD users claim that it makes sex more pleasurable and orgasms more intense and prolonged, the fact is that LSD's main effects, including the intense preoccupation with self that often accompanies an LSD "trip," usually preclude intimate contact with another person. Therefore, while the user is feeling erotic, he or she is content to sit and ponder this stimulation, feeling no compulsion to act upon it.

The ability of LSD to interfere with or grossly distort the senses also presents a unique set of problems to the user. Distortions of the sense of touch and alterations in depth perception can make any physical encounter disorienting, even frightening. And LSD, with its derangement of the sense of self, can make it very difficult for adolescents and adults alike to make responsible decisions about sexual conduct.

•Methaqualone, Barbiturates, and other Depressants. Those who search for love potions seem to many to have a confused sense of direction. In pursuit of heightened sexual pleasure, they may chase such "uppers" as amphetamine and cocaine, or, with equal conviction of success, "downers."

"Downer" is a popular street name for a large group of drugs that includes sedatives, hypnotics (sleeping pills), and antianxiety agents. The most frequently prescribed and used drugs in the United States, downers — despite chemical differences — all appear to work in a similar fashion in the brain, producing a drowsy euphoria, emotional swings, and other similar effects. But there are large differences in the speed with which they take effect and how long they last.

Among the best known of these drugs are barbiturates (phenobarbital, Seconal); benzodiazepines (Valium, Librium, Dalmane) and the so-called nonbarbiturate sedatives Miltown and Equanil (meprobamate) and methaqualone (Quaalude).

The medical uses of these drugs are numerous — in stroke victims' muscle spasms, cerebral palsy, back pain, delirium tremens (convulsions brought on by withdrawal from alcohol), serious anxiety disorders, pain, and insomnia. Studies over the past decade have begun to show that these drugs connect with specific receptors in the brain and possibly mimic natural brain chemicals that help regulate our emotions and moods.

Their potential for abuse and danger, however, is as high as the rate at which they are prescribed or illegally purchased. Physical addiction, born of tolerance and physical dependence, can occur with all of these drugs. Withdrawal brings on weakness, nausea, vomiting, cramps, delirium, and even convulsions. The very conditions these drugs were created to stop — anxiety and excitability — appear in concentrated form when the drug is withdrawn.

Acute overdoses can produce slurred speech, bad judgment, and psychotic behavior. Worse, in the case of the barbiturates, the dose needed to kill a user is not much higher than the amount he or she needs to feel "high," and the lethal dose is not much different in addicts than in a first-time user.

Samples of blotter acid, or squares of blotter paper saturated with LSD. LSD grossly distorts depth perception and the sense of touch, and it can thus make sexual encounters disorienting and even frightening.

Today, the risks of use are so heavy that these drugs are legally available only by prescription; methaqualone can be used for research purposes only. Nevertheless, the reputation of sedative/hypnotics, particularly barbiturates and methaqualone, as aphrodisiacs has persisted among the young since the 1960s.

The reason is not hard to find. Like alcohol and to some extent marijuana, sedative hypnotic drugs turn down the nerve-firing activity of brain cells but turn up the sexual response by lowering the higher brain centers' control over inhibitions and anxiety and relaxing muscles.

None, however, outranks the reputation of methaqualone. First used in medical practice in 1950 in India, methaqualone came to the United States in 1965 under the Quaalude brand name as a sleeping pill and daytime sedative.

Scientists believed that the drug's chemical differences from barbiturates would prevent the addiction and dependence problems patients had with other sedatives, and federal regulators did not see a need for strict control of the drug.

Within a few years, however, overdoses and street abuse, leading to addiction, were reported worldwide. In the 1960s, the hippie counterculture selected methaqualone as its downer and aphrodisiac of choice. Users claimed the erotic properties it triggered were similar to those of marijuana, but more intense.

By the 1970s, Quaalude was widely abused on college campuses, where it earned the label the "love drug." Users frequently mentioned that "ludes" (as they were popularly known) brought on a tingling sensation all over their bodies, especially in women.

Scientists and sexologists had little time before the drug was declared illegal to study its aphrodisiac potential. But most experts believe the drug works only indirectly — by reducing inhibitions — and not directly on sexual activity centers in the brain or genitals.

Studies show that methaqualone, even in moderate or low doses, produces effects so similar to alcohol that, in 1981 alone, methaqualone was implicated in an estimated 20% of all traffic deaths in some areas of the United States. Tolerance to the drug develops rapidly, leading users to crave higher doses; overdoses present unusual and serious medical emergencies. Treatment is complicated by the fact that today, almost all of the drug sold illegally comes from inconsistent and potentially contaminated South American sources.

The classic barbiturate sedatives had their origins in barbituric acid, first made in 1862 by the same German chemist whose company later synthesized aspirin and heroin, Adolph Bayer. Addiction to the drugs was recorded at the turn of the century, but their widespread abuse and real danger were not really recognized until 50 years later. From the 1950s through the 1970s barbiturates figured widely in many of the sex and drug scandals involving Hollywood celebrities, and in the deaths of many stars living at the edge of their feelings and the top of their energy.

Searching for drugs that would reduce anxiety without sedation, scientists developed the benzodiazepines, notably diazepam, (the generic name for Valium). According to pharmaceutical industry sources, diazepam is the most widely prescribed drug in the world. Taken in large doses over long periods of time Valium also produces sedation by depressing the brain's breathing control center. However, the drug can reduce anxiety in doses that do not sedate.

It is no surprise, then, that the characteristics of barbiturate drugs — reduced anxiety, drowsiness, loss of inhibitions, and a feeling of well-being — are sought by many to aid in sexual arousal and enhancement of romantic moments. But again, like alcohol, they produce a two-sided effect: initially, a positive effect on sexual desire, followed by decreased performance. In the final analysis, "downers," like "uppers," exact a sometimes lethal price when used to help initiate, prolong, or enhance sexual performance.

Overall, psychoactive drugs make sexual promises they are unable to keep. Though some may lower inhibitions, or increase desire, there is usually a trade-off in performance. In some cases, there is even permanent damage to sexuality, fertility, and reproduction. Taking into account the poor performance, and the risk of permanent sexual dysfunction, it is easy to recognize that the risks and dangers involved with illicit drug experimentation far outweigh any temporary pleasurable effects they are able to produce.

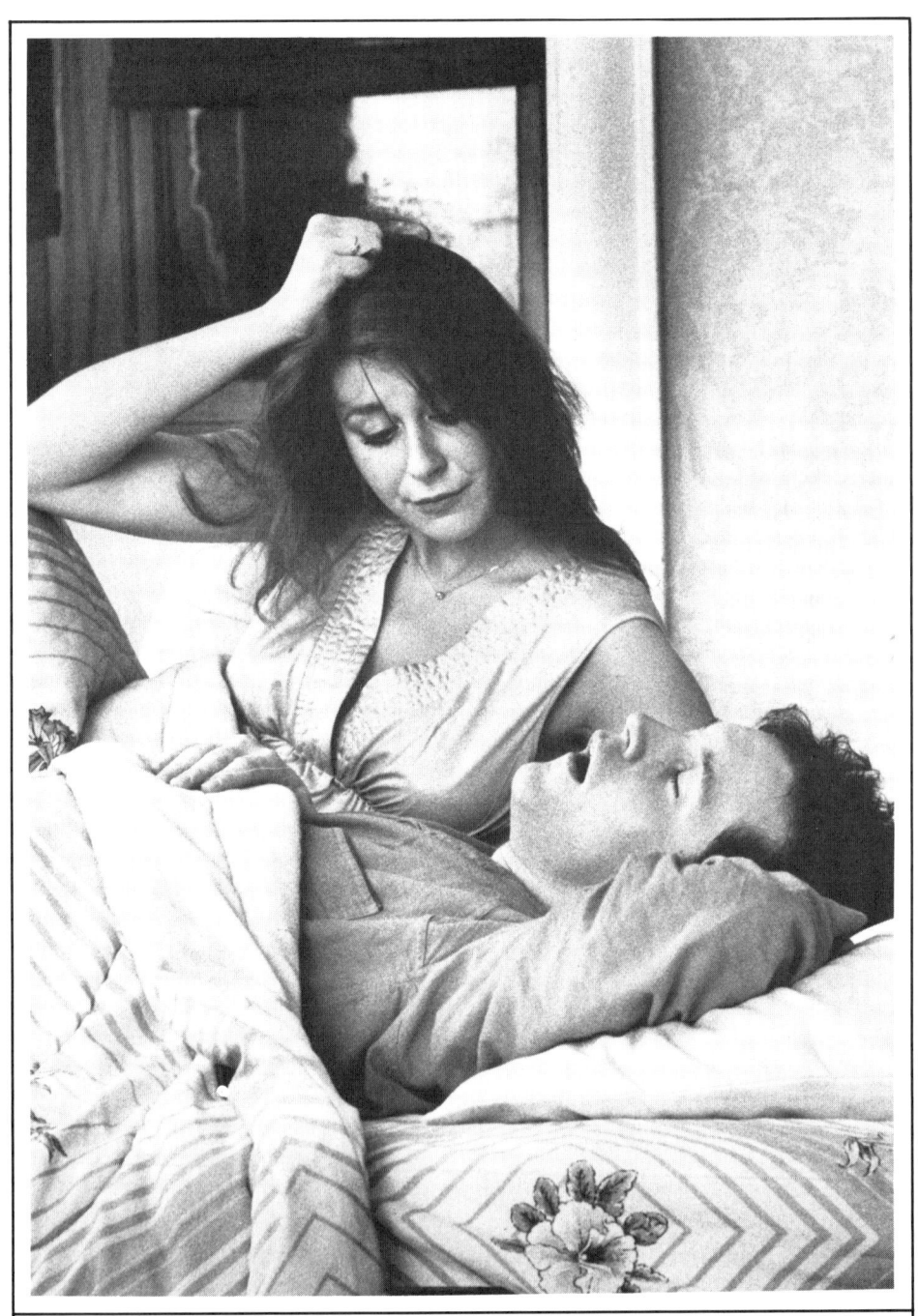

Many people — both men and women — experience problems with sexual arousal and performance at one time or another. In most cases these problems are temporary and can be easily treated.

CHAPTER 5

SEXUAL PROBLEMS: PHYSIOLOGICAL AND PSYCHOLOGICAL

What many people think of as sexual dysfunction or malfunction is usually simply part of the normal variation in human sexuality, a reflection of cultural and personal differences and preferences in the wide range of sexual activities. Not all sexual encounters are equally satisfying or successful. At one time or another most people have anxiety about sexual performance or the degree of arousal they can achieve. Some worry if the attractions they feel for others are "normal," particularly if it is for someone of the same sex. Others are concerned that they think about sex too much or too little. Even in the best relationships, there are those times when one or both partners feel sexually dissatisfied and wonder whether or not this indicates some serious problem.

Myths about sexual abnormalities are abundant. One such myth, for example, is that all normal teenagers think about sex — wild sex — rather continuously. Yet if teenagers are frank with each other, they soon learn that this is simply not the case. It is perfectly normal for teenagers to have long periods of time when sex is not particularly compelling and when nonsexual activities are far more appealing.

There are, of course, real cases of sexual dysfunction, of impotence (the inability to get or sustain an erection) in males and frigidity (the inability to become sexually aroused) in females. But for otherwise normal young people, such instances are extremely rare; when they do occur they are the result of or associated with injuries or illnesses. Sooner or later, just about everyone who is biologically capable can, if they work at it, experience peak sexual pleasure, including orgasm.

Adolescence is a time of change, both physically and psychologically, and such periods of change are not always conducive to creating and maintaining a good environment for "perfect" sexual expression. In formal and informal sessions with teenagers, experts have learned that for many teens, sexual intercourse is far from the "earth moving" romantic or physical experience they have been led to expect. Unfortunately, when sex fails to meet their expectations, some teens then turn to drugs to provide them with sexual fulfillment or in an attempt to medicate themselves for the sexual problems they believe they are experiencing.

In most cases, however, it is simply the fear and anxiety that go hand-in-hand with inexperience and lack of emotional readiness that are masquerading as symptoms of sexual difficulties. That is, most teenagers encounter problems with sex from time to time, but most often, these problems are not because of a serious or incurable condition.

Some Common Sexual Problems

•Painful intercourse. In females, the usual causes for painful intercourse are a vaginal opening that is not stretched enough to take an erect penis; lack of lubrication due to insufficient arousal; vaginal infection; and anxiety. All of these conditions are treatable or preventable. The vaginal opening can be gradually stretched with fingers or by a physician in a simple, painless operation. Lubricants available at the local drug store can help. Infections can be diagnosed and treated with antibiotics or other medications. Anxiety requires time, patience, and, in some cases, discussion with a professional counselor.

Males, too, can have pain during intercourse. It is usually due to an infection or local irritation.

SEXUAL PROBLEMS: PHYSIOLOGICAL AND PSYCHOLOGICAL

•Inability to reach climax. Females often have trouble reaching orgasm, especially if they are sexually inexperienced. They are often more inhibited about telling their partners what they prefer, about moving their bodies in particular ways to increase pleasure, or touching themselves to gain experience. They may also feel it is "unromantic" to ask their partners to do particular things during lovemaking. Most counselors advise women to resist being pressured into sexual intercourse; to go at their own pace; to stop worrying about orgasms and pay more attention to other kinds of sexual pleasure and to work toward relationships in which they are able to communicate their needs and feelings.

If the problem remains serious, however, the woman should seek out a therapist who can help her work through the problem on an emotional level and also suggest exercises she could try in order to familiarize herself with her body.

The popular assumption that adolescents think constantly about sex is not necessarily accurate. On the contrary, teenagers are often far more interested in nonsexual activities, such as sports or music.

In males, inability to climax takes the form of not being able to ejaculate, technically called retarded ejaculation. This can be caused by feelings of guilt and performance anxiety. Often, this condition can be overcome by talking out the problem, and possibly entering sex therapy. In therapy, the therapist can help the man explore his feelings and suggest techniques for solving his problem.

•Impotence. Failing to get or keep an erection is emotionally painful for men of any age. Because many men feel an erection is the visible sign of their masculinity, simply worrying about whether or not they will be able to get or keep one may actually prevent it from happening. It is worth emphasizing that *all* men have trouble from time to time getting or keeping erections. Frequently, abuse of alcohol and other drugs results in temporary impotence.

A female partner can often help a man to overcome instances of occasional impotence. A warm and caring emotional relationship can reduce any anxieties associated with lovemaking. It also makes it easier to take the focus off intercourse as the only means of sexual pleasure.

If impotence occurs quite often or becomes permanent, professional help should be found. Once again, a qualified sex therapist can help a man discover what is causing his impotence and suggest specific techniques for curing it.

•Premature ejaculation. Climaxing too fast is another problem males experience, particularly in their first sexual experiences or when they make love for the first time with a new partner. Often, premature ejaculation is caused by anxiety or fatigue. However, as Ruth Bell points out in *Changing Bodies, Changing Lives*, what is too fast for one person may be just right for another. "Sex," she says, "is not an endurance test." If the condition is serious, specific techniques for overcoming it might include changing the way the body moves during intercourse, cutting off a particularly exciting fantasy, or actually focusing on controlling the climax.

Chronic premature ejaculation can and should be treated by a therapist. Patients can be taught to control their thoughts and to become aware of their bodies' responses. Also, there are specific exercises they can try with their partners that can help them to prolong pleasure and endurance.

A gay couple in New York City's Greenwich Village. Homosexuality is no longer considered a sexual abnormality but rather an alternate life-style that mature adults sometimes prefer.

Homosexuality

In the past, homosexuality was believed to be "sick" and "perverted" and classified strictly as a mental illness. Many people still believe that homosexuality is wrong for moral or religious reasons, but physicians, scientists, and others are increasingly coming to regard homosexuality as an alternate life-style rather than a sexual deviance.

Today, most people know and understand that 5–10% of the human race is sexually attracted primarily to members of their own sex. They also know that such attractions and feelings are not a mark of sexual abnormality. They recognize that the human sexual experience is a vastly varied one and that human beings have very different sexual needs over their lifetimes. It is not unusual for boys and girls to be "in love" with members of their own sex or to explore their sexuality with the same sex early in their lives. This is not necessarily an indication of homosexuality, but rather is often part of the exploration of different sexual roles. As such it is perfectly normal and no cause for alarm.

Also, it is important to understand that, like heterosexuals, not all gay men and women perform all possible gay sexual acts. Homosexual men and women express their sexuality in as many different ways as heterosexual men and women do.

Adolescents who have homosexual feelings or have experimented with a member of the same sex are not abnormal, crazy, bad, or weird. Those who are disturbed or frightened by these feelings should, by all means, seek some counseling. There are also books available that can provide information, reassurance, and further sources of help.

Since the discovery of Acquired Immune Deficiency Syndrome (AIDS), homosexual relationships have become more feared than ever. Because the disease first began to spread in the homosexual community, many people classified it as a "homosexual disease."

It is important to understand, however, that AIDS is *not* just a "gay" disease; that heterosexual couples can and do contract the disease. The AIDS virus is carried in blood and sexual fluids and can be transmitted during intercourse. Some acts, such as anal intercourse, increase the chances of contracting AIDS from an infected partner. These sexual acts are characterized as high-risk. Promiscuity, as well as sex with any person whose health status is unknown to you, also increases your chances of contracting the disease. Consequently, other than to abstain from sex, the only way to protect yourself from the AIDS virus is to practice "safe sex" — that is, using a condom and spermicide, avoiding high-risk sexual acts, and limiting the number of your sexual partners.

The AIDS virus can also be contracted through the sharing of contaminated needles among intravenous drug abusers, intercourse with an infected intravenous drug user, or sex with an infected partner who has had homosexual relations. Bisexuality, having sex with both members of the opposite sex and members of the same sex, offers a clear danger with regard to the transmission of AIDS. Because many bisexuals — like many heterosexuals — are not monogamous or very open about their sexuality, it is nearly impossible to determine exactly who is a high-risk partner and who is not. Consequently, casual sex can turn into a particularly dangerous, even fatal, practice.

The AIDS virus reaches into all socioeconomic, cultural, and sexual groups. It has struck down housewives, husbands, health care professionals, children, and many others. But even though there is no absolute safeguard against this deadly disease, teenagers can avoid putting themselves at risk by using condoms, avoiding promiscuous behavior, and never using intravenous drugs.

A married couple consults a therapist. Psychotherapists have had a great deal of success in treating sexual dysfunction. Rarely, if ever, are sexual problems treated with therapeutic drugs.

CHAPTER 6

LEGITIMATE DRUG TREATMENT AND SEXUAL THERAPY

Although it is true that there is no drug with the magical power to guarantee great sex, scientists have discovered that certain drugs may be able to restore a normal sex life to those people who through illness have been denied one.

•L-dopa. One of these drugs is levodihydroxyphenylalanine (L-dopa). L-dopa is used to treat Parkinson's disease, a disease of the nervous system usually afflicting elderly people and characterized by tremors, involuntary muscular movements, abnormal slowness of movement, stooping, and muscle rigidity. Parkinson's causes the destruction of neurons in the substantia nigra section of the basal ganglia, located in the brain. The *substantia nigra* — black substance — is so named because to the naked eye it appears that the tissue is black. The *basal ganglia* are actually four clusters of neurons located in the part of the brain concerned with the control of movement.

The neurons in the substantia nigra that are destroyed are responsible for the release of the neurotransmitter dopamine in the brain. The drug L-dopa is used to treat Parkinson's disease because it is transformed into dopamine by the brain.

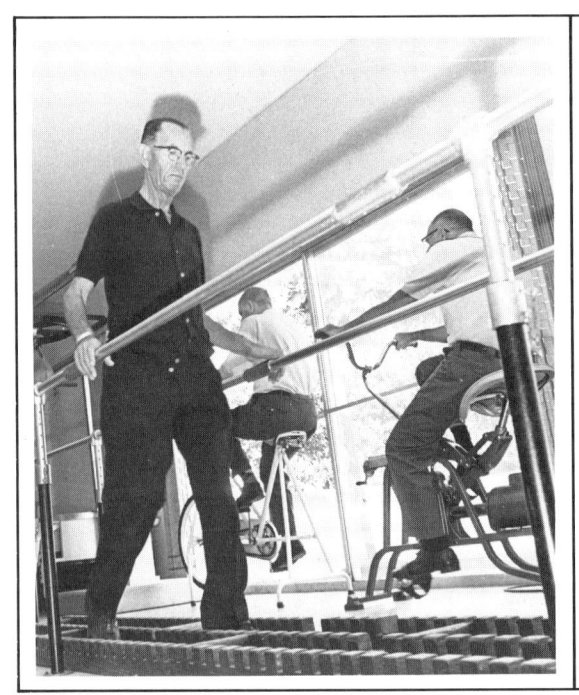

A victim of Parkinson's disease during a physical therapy session. Studies show that L-dopa, a drug used in the treatment of Parkinson's, may be able to restore a normal sex life to people who have been denied one because of illness.

It has also been observed that patients, elderly men in particular, have experienced a kind of sexual rejuvenation while taking L-dopa. Although L-dopa later proved to have a similar effect on younger men suffering from sexual dysfunction, the effect was short-lived and unsatisfactory. So, though L-dopa is not an aphrodisiac, and does not work on healthy males, or even on those suffering from sexual dysfunction, one of its side effects has been to restore sexuality and perhaps add to the quality of life of patients with Parkinson's disease.

•Bromocriptine. Another drug that may have an effect on sexuality is bromocriptine, a fertility drug that acts on a gland at the base of the brain. Scientists in Europe have discovered that a few women taking the drug have reported that their interest in sex has increased. This drug, which is known to cause serious side effects, is not available in the United States.

•Another approach to the treatment of sexual problems is still very much in the experimental stage. It is a nutritional therapy based on a theory posited by Dr. Gian Luigi Gessa, an Italian professor of pharmacology. Dr. Gessa has experimented with a diet free of tryptophan, a nutrient the body needs to make serotonin, a vital brain chemical. In animal studies, Gessa found that a lack of serotonin may trigger hypersexual behavior. Tryptophan is found naturally in milk, cheese, and other dairy products. As of yet, the use of a low-tryptophan diet as an aphrodisiac is just theory.

There are many other scientists and researchers looking to develop a true aphrodisiac. Even perfume companies are getting into the act, with the development of a new line of colognes containing hormones or pheromones to lure the object of your desire. But many of these substances are being developed for commercial use only and have little effect on legitimate research into sexual dysfunction.

Sexual Therapy

One of the most successful treatments of sexual dysfunction has been in the area of sexual therapy. Different practitioners take different approaches, depending on where they believe sexual problems ultimately lie. Sexual therapy can involve talking a problem through; trying to discover if there is an underlying reason for the dysfunction if all biological factors have been ruled out. This can mean going back over childhood experiences to see if there is a particularly disturbing memory that may be inhibiting or destroying sexuality. A sex therapist can also help a patient explore the possibility that unresolved conflicts or problems in a current relationship may be taking a toll on sexual performance.

Sexual therapy may also serve as a forum for delving into particular ingrained social customs or religious beliefs that may be adversely affecting sexuality. It can also provide an opportunity for people who want to unburden themselves to do so. Just as important, a competent sex therapist may have information at his or her disposal that is hard to come by anywhere else.

A professional sex therapist has been trained to address a wide range of psychological issues. He or she can help a patient search out those psychological factors that are harming sexuality and bring them to light. He or she can serve both partners in a relationship at the same time and help open up channels of honest communication. Frequently, sex therapists give their patients a series of practical exercises that, over time, can solve many common sexual problems such as frigidity, impotence, and premature ejaculation.

The ages-old search for substances that heighten sexual pleasure continues. Most people agree, however, that the safest — and by far the best — aphrodisiac is a natural, healthy, loving relationship.

CHAPTER 7

CONCLUSION

As we have seen, the search for aphrodisiacs is ages old. But the herbal potions and magic rites known to ancient cultures are a far cry from some of the potent drugs available today. Today, as in the past, drugs reputed to have aphrodisiac effects may cause drowsiness, nausea, or have no effect at all. But there are others that offer the risks of permanent brain damage, cardiac arrest, coma, and death. At the very least, these drugs may cause temporary or permanent problems in the sexual performance teenagers hope they will enhance.

Teenagers are particularly vulnerable to drugs that seem to offer solutions to the problems of sexuality. In the search for what they think will be better sex, teens may turn to drugs that in fact bring with them dangerous physical and emotional consequences. What people should bear in mind is that aphrodisiacs and psychoactive drugs falsely presumed to be sexual enhancers ultimately offer little more than the deadening of the very pleasure they were meant to heighten.

A young woman receives information about birth control at a clinic. Health professionals hope that birth control information will help lower the rate of unwanted pregnancies in the United States.

EDITORS' NOTE

A WORD ABOUT BIRTH CONTROL

Because this is a book that deals in large part with teenage sexuality, readers may want some information about ways to help control the epidemic of teenage pregnancy.

Although chemical substances used for birth control are not psychoactive agents, they have had a revolutionary influence on sexual behavior. In the contemporary world, "the pill" has become the single most significant drug involved in human sexuality. Advanced birth control techniques ushered in an era of supposedly worry-free sex during the 1960s and 1970s, seeming to assure, as they then did, "liberation" from the consequences of unwanted pregnancy.

For the purposes of a straightforward discussion of chemical agents used in birth control, let us leave aside for the time being the fact that the AIDS epidemic has given the lie to the possibility of divorcing sexuality from potentially dangerous consequences. The fact remains that the statistics on unwanted pregnancies in the United States are staggering and that this national crisis is at least in part ascribable to the fact that even those young people who have been adequately educated on available methods of birth control are chosing for whatever reason not to use them.

According to the U.S. Department of Health and Human Services, in 1978 alone almost half of the 545,000 babies born out of wedlock were born to teenage mothers. The department also reports that among sexually active 15 year olds, less than one-third used any form of contraceptive at the time of first intercourse.

Many teenagers, and adults as well, shun the use of birth control in an attempt to cope with feelings of ambivalence about the fact that they are sexually active in the first place. The rationale goes something like this: If I use birth control, I am admitting that I engage in behavior that at least on some level makes me feel anxious and guilty. If I avoid using birth control, it is easier for me to deny these feelings. These people, unable to deal with their confusion, are often blind to the consequences of unwanted pregnancy and the dangers of contracting sexually transmitted diseases.

Other people, willing to use methods of contraception, nonetheless fail to realize that the birth control pill and various spermicidal creams and foams must be used according to very specific directions. There is no "magic" to any form of birth control — sporadic or improper use will in all likelihood render them useless.

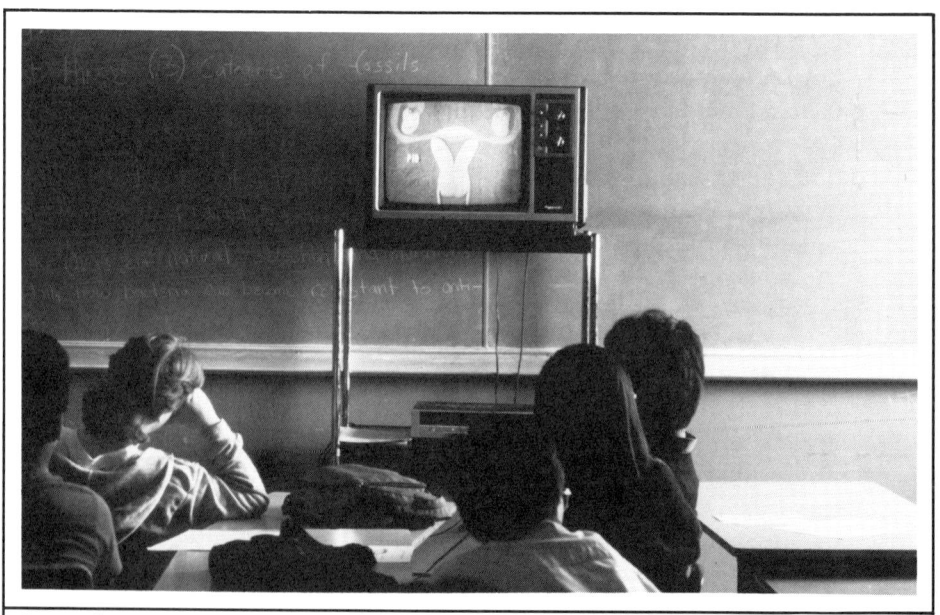

Sex education classes, which are taught in almost every high school in the United States, often show video displays of the female and male reproductive systems as part of the discussion on birth control.

The many forms of chemical birth control available today vary widely in terms of safety and effectiveness. Although most can prevent unwanted pregnancy if taken as directed, many offer no protection against sexually transmitted diseases; still others can have adverse side effects on the health of the user. The following is a consideration of the most widely used and available chemical forms of birth control.

•Oral Contraceptives. More commonly known as "the pill," oral contraceptives are taken by the woman and contain a combination of real or synthetic hormones used to prevent ovulation (the time during a woman's menstrual cycle when the ovum, or egg, breaks through the ovary walls and enters the fallopian tubes). This makes it impossible for fertilization, or conception, to take place.

The early pill's many serious side effects began to manifest themselves very soon after it was introduced to the public during the mid-1950s. Many of the first oral contraceptives contained very high amounts of the hormone estrogen, which appeared to cause medical problems for some users. There were reports of wild mood swings, increased risk of breast cancer and cancer of the female reproductive organs, hormonal imbalances, menstrual difficulties, and a higher mortality rate among users.

Today, oral contraceptives contain much lower doses of estrogen. In fact, the U.S. Department of Health and Human Services recently reported that less than 10% of all oral contraceptives contain 50 micrograms or more of estrogen. Research is under way to discover if estrogen levels in oral contraceptives can be further reduced.

The new low-estrogen pills and mini-pills have far fewer side effects than the pills of the past, but they are not completely danger-free. The high-risk groups — women who smoke; women over 35; women with a family history of blood clots, breast cancer, diabetes, or heart disease — are still discouraged from taking oral contraceptives and are shown to have a higher mortality rate than those women with no risk factors at all. Birth control pills are known to cause blood clots, partial blindness, and stroke in some of their users, along with a host of vaguely uncomfortable side effects. These effects include bloating, weight gain, spotting, nausea, and both decreased and increased sexual interest. (Obviously, the

A clever advertisement serves as a reminder that safe sex is more than a good method of birth control. It can be the difference between life and death.

effects vary from woman to woman, hence the apparent contradiction in effects.)

Today the birth control pill remains one of the most popular forms of contraception available. Although it is not recommended for everyone, it is easily obtained by a doctor's prescription. Prior to her first prescription, and annually thereafter, the woman must submit to a series of blood tests and a physical exam by her physician to determine what, if any, effects the pill has had on her cholesterol levels and general health. Currently the birth control pill is available only to women, although attempts have been made to produce a male version of this popular contraceptive. The first result of this experiment was male impotence. The research continues today.

- Spermicides. Spermicides include vaginal suppositories, foams, jellies, and creams that block the entrance to the uterus and kill sperm. These spermicides are usually introduced into the vaginal area immediately prior to intercourse and must be readministered if intercourse is repeated.

When used with a condom (a thin rubber sheath that fits over the penis), spermicides are very effective (somewhere in the neighborhood of 98%). But when used alone, spermicides have a failure rate of almost 25%.

Several adverse side effects have been noted in connection with the use of spermicides. Although it is true that some may be instrumental in the prevention of contracting some sexually transmitted diseases (including, recent research shows, the deadly AIDS virus, when used with a latex condom), they can also cause irritation of the penis and the vagina. Some users also report that the use of spermicides can be both messy and inconvenient because they must be applied just before intercourse and invariably interrupt foreplay.

A variety of other chemical birth control preparations are currently being researched, and a few are being used in limited situations. Among those that are still being researched but are not approved for general use are the "morning after" pills, which are supposed to be taken sometime between several hours and the third morning after sex has taken place. These drugs, in effect a form of chemical abortion, act either to prevent fertilization of the egg by the sperm or to halt the development of an already fertilized egg.

Progesterone injections, which can block ovulation, are also considered a form of birth control, but these, too, are not widely used. Reasearch is now under way for developing new, improved forms of birth control, including the male pill, nasal sprays, and a long-term time-release device that would be implanted under the skin in the arm and release the contraceptive into the body.

APPENDIX

State Agencies for the Prevention and Treatment of Drug Abuse

ALABAMA
Department of Mental Health
Division of Mental Illness and
  Substance Abuse Community
  Programs
200 Interstate Park Drive
P.O. Box 3710
Montgomery, AL 36193
(205) 271-9253

ALASKA
Department of Health and Social
  Services
Office of Alcoholism and Drug
  Abuse
Pouch H-05-F
Juneau, AK 99811
(907) 586-6201

ARIZONA
Department of Health Services
Division of Behavioral Health
  Services
Bureau of Community Services
Alcohol Abuse and Alcoholism
  Section
2500 East Van Buren
Phoenix, AZ 85008
(602) 255-1238

Department of Health Services
Division of Behavioral Health
  Services
Bureau of Community Services
Drug Abuse Section
2500 East Van Buren
Phoenix, AZ 85008
(602) 255-1240

ARKANSAS
Department of Human Services
Office of Alcohol and Drug Abuse
  Prevention
1515 West 7th Avenue
Suite 310
Little Rock, AR 72202
(501) 371-2603

CALIFORNIA
Department of Alcohol and Drug
  Abuse
111 Capitol Mall
Sacramento, CA 95814
(916) 445-1940

COLORADO
Department of Health
Alcohol and Drug Abuse Division
4210 East 11th Avenue
Denver, CO 80220
(303) 320-6137

CONNECTICUT
Alcohol and Drug Abuse
  Commission
999 Asylum Avenue
3rd Floor
Hartford, CT 06105
(203) 566-4145

DELAWARE
Division of Mental Health
Bureau of Alcoholism and Drug
  Abuse
1901 North Dupont Highway
Newcastle, DE 19720
(302) 421-6101

DISTRICT OF COLUMBIA
Department of Human Services
Office of Health Planning and
  Development
601 Indiana Avenue, NW
Suite 500
Washington, D.C. 20004
(202) 724-5641

FLORIDA
Department of Health and
  Rehabilitative Services
Alcoholic Rehabilitation Program
1317 Winewood Boulevard
Room 187A
Tallahassee, FL 32301
(904) 488-0396

Department of Health and
  Rehabilitative Services
Drug Abuse Program
1317 Winewood Boulevard
Building 6, Room 155
Tallahassee, FL 32301
(904) 488-0900

GEORGIA
Department of Human Resources
Division of Mental Health and
  Mental Retardation
Alcohol and Drug Section
618 Ponce De Leon Avenue, NE
Atlanta, GA 30365-2101
(404) 894-4785

HAWAII
Department of Health
Mental Health Division
Alcohol and Drug Abuse Branch
1250 Punch Bowl Street
P.O. Box 3378
Honolulu, HI 96801
(808) 548-4280

IDAHO
Department of Health and Welfare
Bureau of Preventive Medicine
Substance Abuse Section
450 West State
Boise, ID 83720
(208) 334-4368

ILLINOIS
Department of Mental Health and
  Developmental Disabilities
Division of Alcoholism
160 North La Salle Street
Room 1500
Chicago, IL 60601
(312) 793-2907

Illinois Dangerous Drugs
  Commission
300 North State Street
Suite 1500
Chicago, IL 60610
(312) 822-9860

INDIANA
Department of Mental Health
Division of Addiction Services
429 North Pennsylvania Street
Indianapolis, IN 46204
(317) 232-7816

IOWA
Department of Substance Abuse
505 5th Avenue
Insurance Exchange Building
Suite 202
Des Moines, IA 50319
(515) 281-3641

KANSAS
Department of Social Rehabilitation
Alcohol and Drug Abuse Services
2700 West 6th Street
Biddle Building
Topeka, KS 66606
(913) 296-3925

KENTUCKY
Cabinet for Human Resources
Department of Health Services
Substance Abuse Branch
275 East Main Street
Frankfort, KY 40601
(502) 564-2880

LOUISIANA
Department of Health and Human Resources
Office of Mental Health and Substance Abuse
655 North 5th Street
P.O. Box 4049
Baton Rouge, LA 70821
(504) 342-2565

MAINE
Department of Human Services
Office of Alcoholism and Drug Abuse Prevention
Bureau of Rehabilitation
32 Winthrop Street
Augusta, ME 04330
(207) 289-2781

MARYLAND
Alcoholism Control Administration
201 West Preston Street
Fourth Floor
Baltimore, MD 21201
(301) 383-2977

State Health Department
Drug Abuse Administration
201 West Preston Street
Baltimore, MD 21201
(301) 383-3312

MASSACHUSETTS
Department of Public Health
Division of Alcoholism
755 Boylston Street
Sixth Floor
Boston, MA 02116
(617) 727-1960

Department of Public Health
Division of Drug Rehabilitation
600 Washington Street
Boston, MA 02114
(617) 727-8617

MICHIGAN
Department of Public Health
Office of Substance Abuse Services
3500 North Logan Street
P.O. Box 30035
Lansing, MI 48909
(517) 373-8603

MINNESOTA
Department of Public Welfare
Chemical Dependency Program Division
Centennial Building
658 Cedar Street
4th Floor
Saint Paul, MN 55155
(612) 296-4614

MISSISSIPPI
Department of Mental Health
Division of Alcohol and Drug Abuse
1102 Robert E. Lee Building
Jackson, MS 39201
(601) 359-1297

MISSOURI
Department of Mental Health
Division of Alcoholism and Drug Abuse
2002 Missouri Boulevard
P.O. Box 687
Jefferson City, MO 65102
(314) 751-4942

MONTANA
Department of Institutions
Alcohol and Drug Abuse Division
1539 11th Avenue
Helena, MT 59620
(406) 449-2827

APPENDIX: STATE AGENCIES

NEBRASKA
Department of Public Institutions
Division of Alcoholism and Drug Abuse
801 West Van Dorn Street
P.O. Box 94728
Lincoln, NB 68509
(402) 471-2851, Ext. 415

NEVADA
Department of Human Resources
Bureau of Alcohol and Drug Abuse
505 East King Street
Carson City, NV 89710
(702) 885-4790

NEW HAMPSHIRE
Department of Health and Welfare
Office of Alcohol and Drug Abuse Prevention
Hazen Drive
Health and Welfare Building
Concord, NH 03301
(603) 271-4627

NEW JERSEY
Department of Health
Division of Alcoholism
129 East Hanover Street CN 362
Trenton, NJ 08625
(609) 292-8949

Department of Health
Division of Narcotic and Drug Abuse Control
129 East Hanover Street CN 362
Trenton, NJ 08625
(609) 292-8949

NEW MEXICO
Health and Environment Department
Behavioral Services Division
Substance Abuse Bureau
725 Saint Michaels Drive
P.O. Box 968
Santa Fe, NM 87503
(505) 984-0020, Ext. 304

NEW YORK
Division of Alcoholism and Alcohol Abuse
194 Washington Avenue
Albany, NY 12210
(518) 474-5417

Division of Substance Abuse Services
Executive Park South
Box 8200
Albany, NY 12203
(518) 457-7629

NORTH CAROLINA
Department of Human Resources
Division of Mental Health, Mental Retardation and Substance Abuse Services
Alcohol and Drug Abuse Services
325 North Salisbury Street
Albemarle Building
Raleigh, NC 27611
(919) 733-4670

NORTH DAKOTA
Department of Human Services
Division of Alcoholism and Drug Abuse
State Capitol Building
Bismarck, ND 58505
(701) 224-2767

OHIO
Department of Health
Division of Alcoholism
246 North High Street
P.O. Box 118
Columbus, OH 43216
(614) 466-3543

Department of Mental Health
Bureau of Drug Abuse
65 South Front Street
Columbus, OH 43215
(614) 466-9023

OKLAHOMA
Department of Mental Health
Alcohol and Drug Programs
4545 North Lincoln Boulevard
Suite 100 East Terrace
P.O. Box 53277
Oklahoma City, OK 73152
(405) 521-0044

OREGON
Department of Human Resources
Mental Health Division
Office of Programs for Alcohol and
  Drug Problems
2575 Bittern Street, NE
Salem, OR 97310
(503) 378-2163

PENNSYLVANIA
Department of Health
Office of Drug and Alcohol
  Programs
Commonwealth and Forster Avenues
Health and Welfare Building
P.O. Box 90
Harrisburg, PA 17108
(717) 787-9857

RHODE ISLAND
Department of Mental Health,
  Mental Retardation and Hospitals
Division of Substance Abuse
Substance Abuse Administration
  Building
Cranston, RI 02920
(401) 464-2091

SOUTH CAROLINA
Commission on Alcohol and Drug
  Abuse
3700 Forest Drive
Columbia, SC 29204
(803) 758-2521

SOUTH DAKOTA
Department of Health
Division of Alcohol and Drug Abuse
523 East Capitol, Joe Foss Building
Pierre, SD 57501
(605) 773-4806

TENNESSEE
Department of Mental Health and
  Mental Retardation
Alcohol and Drug Abuse Services
505 Deaderick Street
James K. Polk Building,
  Fourth Floor
Nashville, TN 37219
(615) 741-1921

TEXAS
Commission on Alcoholism
809 Sam Houston State Office
  Building
Austin, TX 78701
(512) 475-2577
Department of Community Affairs
Drug Abuse Prevention Division
2015 South Interstate Highway 35
P.O. Box 13166
Austin, TX 78711
(512) 443-4100

UTAH
Department of Social Services
Division of Alcoholism and Drugs
150 West North Temple
Suite 350
P.O. Box 2500
Salt Lake City, UT 84110
(801) 533-6532

VERMONT
Agency of Human Services
Department of Social and
  Rehabilitation Services
Alcohol and Drug Abuse Division
103 South Main Street
Waterbury, VT 05676
(802) 241-2170

APPENDIX: STATE AGENCIES

VIRGINIA
Department of Mental Health and
  Mental Retardation
Division of Substance Abuse
109 Governor Street
P.O. Box 1797
Richmond, VA 23214
(804) 786-5313

WASHINGTON
Department of Social and Health
  Service
Bureau of Alcohol and Substance
  Abuse
Office Building—44 W
Olympia, WA 98504
(206) 753-5866

WEST VIRGINIA
Department of Health
Office of Behavioral Health Services
Division on Alcoholism and Drug
  Abuse
1800 Washington Street East
Building 3 Room 451
Charleston, WV 25305
(304) 348-2276

WISCONSIN
Department of Health and Social
  Services
Division of Community Services
Bureau of Community Programs
Alcohol and Other Drug Abuse
  Program Office
1 West Wilson Street
P.O. Box 7851
Madison, WI 53707
(608) 266-2717

WYOMING
Alcohol and Drug Abuse Programs
Hathaway Building
Cheyenne, WY 82002
(307) 777-7115, Ext. 7118

GUAM
Mental Health & Substance Abuse
  Agency
P.O. Box 20999
Guam 96921

PUERTO RICO
Department of Addiction Control
  Services
Alcohol Abuse Programs
P.O. Box B-Y Rio Piedras Station
Rio Piedras, PR 00928
(809) 763-5014

Department of Addiction Control
  Services
Drug Abuse Programs
P.O. Box B-Y Rio Piedras Station
Rio Piedras, PR 00928
(809) 764-8140

VIRGIN ISLANDS
Division of Mental Health,
  Alcoholism & Drug Dependency
  Services
P.O. Box 7329
Saint Thomas, Virgin Islands 00801
(809) 774-7265

AMERICAN SAMOA
LBJ Tropical Medical Center
Department of Mental Health Clinic
Pago Pago, American Samoa 96799

TRUST TERRITORIES
Director of Health Services
Office of the High Commissioner
Saipan, Trust Territories 96950

Further Reading

Ashley, Richard. *Cocaine: Its History, Uses and Effects.* New York: St. Martin's Press, 1975.

Belkin, G. S. *Contemporary Psychotherapies.* Chicago: Rand McNally, 1980.

Bell, Ruth. *Changing Bodies, Changing Lives.* New York: Random House, 1980.

Calderone, Mary S., M.D. *Manual of Family Planning and Contraceptive Practice.* 2d edition. Melbourne, FL: Krieger, 1970.

Calderone, Mary S., M.D., and Eric W. Johnson. *The Family Book About Sexuality.* New York: Harper & Row, 1981.

Durden-Smith, Jo, and Diane Desimone. *Sex and the Brain.* New York: Arbor House, 1983.

Encyclopaedia Britannica. *Medical Health Annual.* Chicago: Encyclopaedia Britannica, 1983.

Kaplan, Helen S., M.D. *The New Sex Therapy.* New York: Quadrangle/The New York Times Book Co., 1974.

Kelly, Gary F. *Learning About Sex: The Contemporary Guide for Young Adults.* New York: Barron's Educational Series, 1977.

Masters, William H., and Virginia Johnson. *Human Sexual Inadequacy.* Boston: Little, Brown, 1970.

Masters, William H., and Virginia Johnson. *Human Sexual Response.* Boston: Little, Brown, 1966.

Money, John, and A. Ehrhardt. *A Man and a Woman, Boy and Girl.* Baltimore: Johns Hopkins University Press, 1972.

Money, John, and Patricia Tucker. *Sexual Signatures: On Being a Man or a Woman.* Boston: Little, Brown, 1975.

Glossary

addiction a condition caused by repeated drug use, characterized by a compulsive urge to continue using the drug, a tendency to increase the dosage, and physiological and/or psychological dependence

AIDS Acquired Immune Deficiency Syndrome; a weakening of the body's immune system caused by a virus (HIV); thought to be spread by blood or sexual contact

alcohol any of a series of hydroxyl compounds that includes ethanol and methanol; the intoxicating agent in liquor

amphetamine a drug that stimulates the central nervous system, generally used as an energizer, antidepressant, or appetite suppressant

androgen one of several principally male sex hormones; the main androgen is testosterone, which controls the development of male sex organs

aphrodisiac a substance thought to arouse sexual desire when ingested

barbiturate a drug that causes depression of the central nervous system; generally used to reduce anxiety or to treat insomnia

basal ganglia four clusters of neurons at the base of the brain, involved in the regulation of movement

cantharides (Spanish Fly) an alleged aphrodisiac made from the coating of a beetle

central nervous system the brain and spinal cord

clitoris a small sex organ in the female located at the opening of the vagina

cocaine the primary psychoactive ingredient in the coca plant and a behavioral stimulant

condom a thin rubber sheath that fits over the penis and is used to prevent pregnancy; offers protection from sexually transmitted diseases

depression a mental condition characterized by sadness, dejection, and apathy

estrogen the principal female sex hormone

ginseng a plant with a fork-shaped root believed to have medicinal properties

hashish an extract prepared from the flowers, stalks, leaves, and resin of the hemp, or marijuana plant, which is smoked for its euphoric effects

hermaphrodite a person who is born with the sexual organs and hormonal potential of both sexes, due to abnormal prenatal development

hormone a chemical released into the bloodstream from special glands such as the thyroid or pituitary gland. Hormones travel throughout the body to activate receptors located on specific organs; they affect the development of glands and can affect sexual drive. At puberty, the secretion by the ovaries of estrogen and progesterone starts and controls menstruation

hypothalamus a region at the base of the brain involved in the regulation of thirst, hunger, sex drive, and body temperature; also plays a vital role in governing the endocrine system and the emotions

LSD lysergic acid diethylamide; a hallucinogen derived from the ergot fungus that grows on rye or from morning glory seeds

marijuana the crushed leaves, flowers, and branches of the hemp plant, containing the psychoactive ingredient tetrahydrocannabinol (THC)

methaqualone generic name of Quaaludes; a nonbarbiturate sedative hypnotic

neurotransmitter a chemical released by neurons that transmits nerve impulses across a synapse

nutmeg *myristica fragrans*; a spice that, when consumed in large amounts, can cause psychoactive effects similar to those of amphetamines, including hyperactivity, agitation, sleeplessness, and nausea; after several hours, the user may experience euphoria and visual hallucinations

oral contraception "the Pill"; a birth control method in which a combination of natural and/or synthetic hormones are used to prevent ovulation in the female

ovulation the time during a female's menstrual cycle when the ovum, or egg, breaks through the ovary walls and enters the fallopian tubes

Parkinson's disease a disease of the nervous system usually affecting the elderly and characterized by tremors, involuntary muscular movement, and muscle rigidity

penis the male sex organ

pheromone a chemical substance an animal releases that elicits certain behavior in others of the same species; often a signal of fertility in female animals

physical dependence an adaptation of the body to the presence of a drug such that the drug's absence produces withdrawal symptoms

pituitary gland a gland that produces various hormones that regulate such bodily functions as growth and reproduction

progesterone a steroid hormone found in women and affecting the menstrual cycle, the development of the maternal placenta, and the mammary glands

psychological dependence a condition in which the drug user craves a drug to maintain a sense of well-being and feels discomfort when deprived of it

puberty the stage in human physical development in which sexual reproduction can first occur; marked by changes in body development

serotonin a compound thought to act as a neurotransmitter affecting sleep functions; widely distributed throughout the body, it acts similarly to the histamines in combating inflammation

spermicides vaginal suppositories, creams, jellies, and foams that block the entrance to the uterus and kill sperm

stimulant any drug that increases brain activity and produces a sensation of greater energy, euphoria, and increased alertness

strychnine an extract from the plant *nux vomica*; a deadly poison usually used to kill rodents

synapse the narrow gap between neurons; the point at which a nerve impulse is transmitted from one neuron to another

testicles two glands in the male that produce male hormones and sperm

testosterone the principal male sex hormone

tolerance a decrease in susceptibility to the effects of a drug due to its continued administration, resulting in the user's need to increase the drug dosage in order to achieve the effects that were previously experienced

vagina the elastic canal in the female extending down from the uterus to an opening in the vulva

withdrawal the psychological and physical effects of the discontinued use of a drug

yohimbine an alkaloid substance chemically related to LSD

PICTURE CREDITS

AP/Wide World Photos: p. 68; Norman Barker/Johns Hopkins School of Medicine: p. 40; The Bettmann Archive: pp. 12, 63; Cindy Charles/Gamma Liaison: p. 74; Culver Pictures: p. 44; Stephen L. Feldman/Photo Researchers, Inc.: p. 46; Charles Marden Fitch/Taurus Photos: p. 55; Mimi Forsyth/Monkmeyer Press Photo Service: pp. 8, 66; Spencer Grant/Photo Researchers, Inc.: p. 32; Jill Hartley/Photo Researchers, Inc.: p. 47; Yvonne Hemsey/Gamma Liaison: p. 72; Chester Higgins, Jr./Photo Researchers, Inc.: p. 70; Mike Kagan/Monkmeyer Press Photo Service: p. 18; Eric Kroll/Taurus Photos: p. 38; Ed Lettau/Photo Researchers, Inc.: pp. 22, 58; Manning/Sygma: p. 37; Tom McHugh/Photo Researchers, Inc.: p. 30; Ira Nyman/Sygma: p. 25; Courtesy of the Oslo Museum: cover; H. Armstrong Roberts: p. 10; Horst Schaffer/Peter Arnold, Inc.: p. 61; Gordon S. Smith/Photo Researchers, Inc.: p. 42; Erika Stone/Photo Researchers, Inc. p. 24; Joseph Szabo/Photo Researchers, Inc.: p. 34; Allan Tannenbaum/Sygma: pp. 50, 52; Original Illustrations by Gary Tong: pp. 26, 28, 29

Index

Acquired Immunodeficiency Syndrome. *See* AIDS
Adolescence
    birth control and, 74
    changes during, 19, 60
    discomfort about sexuality, 20, 60, 73
    drug use during, 19–20, 49, 55–57, 60, 71
    homosexuality and, 64
    pregnancy during, 73–74
    sexual intercourse during, 20, 60
    sexual maturation, 19
Adrenal cortex, 36. *See also* Sex hormones
Adrenal glands, 36. *See also* Sex hormones
AIDS (Acquired Immunodeficiency Syndrome), 64–65, 73
Alcohol. *See also* Aphrodisiacs; Drugs, psychoactive
    as aphrodisiac, 19, 21, 45–49
    impotence and, 47
    methaqualone and, 56
    physiological effects, 45–47
    psychological effects, 46–48
    sexual performance and, 46–49
Amphetamines, 45, 53. *See also* Aphrodisiacs; Drugs, psychoactive
Androgens, 35–40. *See also* Sex hormones
Aphrodisiacs. *See also* Drugs, psychoactive; Sex; Sexual arousal
    definition, 43
    history, 20–21, 43, 71
    misconceptions about, 20–21, 43–49, 57, 71
    psychoactive drugs as, 51–57
    risks, 43–49, 51–57, 71
    sex hormones, 34, 39–41
    substances used as, 20–21, 44–49, 51–57
Aphrodite, 21
Aspirin, 20, 56

Barbiturates, 54–57. *See also* Aphrodisiacs; Drugs, psychoactive
Barbituric acid, 56. *See also* Barbiturates
Basal ganglia, 67
Bayer, Adolph, 56
Bell, Ruth, 23, 62
Benzodiazepines, 54, 56. *See also* Aphrodisiacs; Drugs, psychoactive
Birth control, 73–77. *See also* Adolescence; Sex
Birth control pill. *See* Oral contraceptives
Bromocriptine, 68

Calderone, Mary, 48
Cantharides (Spanish Fly), 44. *See also* Aphrodisiacs
Changing Bodies, Changing Lives (Bell), 23, 62
Cholesterol, 76
Chromosomes, 52
Climax, 24–25, 27, 46. *See also* Orgasms; Sexual arousal
    inability to reach, 61–62
Clitoris, 26–27. *See also* Sexual arousal
Cocaine, 19, 52–53. *See also* Aphrodisiacs; Drugs, psychoactive
Condoms, 77. *See also* Birth control

Dalmane, 54. *See also* Aphrodisiacs; Drugs, psychoactive
Department of Health and Human Services, U.S., 73, 75
Diazepam. *See* Valium
Dopamine, 53, 67
"Downer," 54, 57
Drugs, psychoactive. *See also* Aphrodisiacs
    addiction, 54, 56
    overdoses, 55–56
    risks, 20, 51–57, 64–65
    sex and, 19–20, 51–57
Ehrhardt, Anke, 36

INDEX

Ejaculation, 28. *See also* Sex, dysfunction; Sexual arousal
   premature, 62, 69
Ejaculatory duct, 28
Endocrine system, 35, 52. *See also* Sex hormones
Equanil (meprobamate), 54. *See also* Aphrodisiacs; Drugs, psychoactive
Estrogen, 33, 36–40, 75. *See also* Birth control; Sex hormones
Excitement, 27. *See also* Sexual arousal

Family Book About Sexuality, The (Calderone), 48
Follicle stimulating hormone (FSH), 36
Frigidity, 60, 69. *See also* Sex, dysfunction
FSH. *See* Follicle stimulating hormone

Gessa, Gian Luigi, 68–69
Ginseng, 45. *See also* Aphrodisiacs

Hashish, 51. *See also* Marijuana
Hermaphrodites, 39. *See also* Sex hormones
Heroin, 56
Homosexuality, 63–64
Hormones. *See* Sex hormones
Hypnotics, 54–56. *See also* Aphrodisiacs; Drugs, psychoactive
Hypothalamus, 33–36. *See also* Sex hormones

Impotence, 26, 47, 60, 62, 69, 76. *See also* Sex, dysfunction

Johnson, Virginia, 24

Kaplan, Helen Singer, 26–27, 35
Kinsey, Alfred, 21

L-dopa, 67–68
LH. *See* Luteinizing hormone
Librium, 54. *See also* Aphrodisiacs; Drugs, psychoactive
Limbic system, 35. *See also* Sex hormones
"Love drugs," 34, 56. *See also* Aphrodisiacs; Drugs, psychoactive
"Love potions," 21, 54. *See also* Aphrodisiacs
LSD, 45, 53–54. *See also* Aphrodisiacs; Drugs, psychoactive

"Ludes." *See* methaqualone
Luteinizing hormone (LH), 36

Marijuana, 19–20, 51–52. *See also* Aphrodisiacs; Drugs, psychoactive
Masters, William, 24
Masturbation, 25–26. *See also* Sexual arousal
Menopause, 40. *See also* Sex hormones
Menstrual cycle, 33, 36–37, 52, 75. *See also* Sex hormones
Meprobamate. *See* Equanil
Methaqualone (Quaalude), 54–56. *See also* Aphrodisiacs; Drugs, psychoactive
Miltown, 54. *See also* Aphrodisiacs; Drugs, psychoactive
Money, John, 31, 36, 40, 48
"Morning after" pill, 77. *See also* Birth control
Myristica fragrans. *See* Nutmeg

Neurotransmitter, 53
Nipples, 27. *See also* Sexual arousal
Norepinephrine, 53
Nutmeg (*Myristica fragrans*), 45. *See also* Aphrodisiacs
Nux vomica, 45. *See also* Strychnine

Oral contraceptives, 75–76. *See also* Birth control
Orgasms, 24–29, 35, 38, 48, 51, 53. *See also* Climax; Sexual arousal
Ovaries, 35–36. *See also* Sex hormones
Ovulation, 75. *See also* Birth control
Ovum, 75

Parkinson's disease, 67–68
Penis, 27–28. *See also* Sexual arousal
Phenobarbital, 54. *See also* Barbiturates
Pheromones, 30, 69. *See also* Sexual arousal
Pituitary gland, 33, 36. *See also* Sex hormones; Sexual arousal
Placenta, 37
Plateau, 24–25, 27. *See also* Sexual arousal
Pleasure centers, 34–35. *See also* Sexual arousal
Primates, 35

91

Progesterone, 36–37, 77. *See also* Birth control; Sexual arousal
Puberty, 19, 36

Quaalude. *See* Methaqualone

Refractory period, 29. *See also* Sexual arousal
Relaxation 24–25, 28. *See also* Sexual arousal
Resolution, 28. *See also* Sexual arousal

Seconal, 54. *See also* Barbiturates
Sedatives, 54–57. *See also* Aphrodisiacs; Drugs, psychoactive
Serotonin, 69
Sex. *See also* Sex hormones; Sexual arousal; Sexuality
   drugs and, 19, 24, 44–49, 51–57, 67–69
   dysfunction, 21, 57, 59–62, 67–69
   function, 29–30
   hormones and, 33
   media and, 21, 23, 48–49
   misconceptions about, 20–21, 34, 59
   therapy, 20, 62, 67–69
Sex flush, 27
Sex hormones. *See also* Sex; Sexual arousal
   as aphrodisiacs, 34, 39–41
   classification, 35–37
   factors affecting, 36
   functions, 33, 35–39
   risks, 41
   sex drive and, 33–34, 36–39
   sexuality and, 33–34
   steroid, 36
   synthesis, 35
Sexual arousal. *See also* Sex
   brain and, 33–35
   cultural factors, 26–27, 31
   drugs and, 44–49
   hormones and, 33–34, 36–41
   individual variations, 25
   male-female differences, 25–29
   pheromones, 30
   physiological events during, 26–29
   pleasure centers and, 35
   psychological factors, 27, 31
   regulation, 34–35
   stages of, 24–29
   stimuli causing, 25, 29–31
Sexual intercourse, 25
   pain during, 60
Sexuality, 23–27, 59–60, 63–64
Sexual revolution, 19, 73
Spanish Fly. *See* Cantharides
Spermicides, 77. *See also* Birth control
Strychnine, 45. *See also* Aphrodisiacs
Substantia nigra, 67

Testes, 35–36. *See also* Sex hormones
Testosterone, 33, 35–36, 38–39, 51. *See also* Sex hormones
THC, 51. *See also* Marijuana
Tryptophan, 68–69

"Uppers," 54, 57. *See also* Aphrodisiacs; Drugs, psychoactive
Uterus, 27, 37

Vagina, 26–27. *See also* Sexual arousal
Valium (diazepam), 54, 56–57. *See also* Aphrodisiacs; Drugs, psychoactive
Vasocongestion, 26. *See also* Sexual arousal
Vitamin E, 20. *See also* Aphrodisiacs

Wilsnack, Sharon C., 45
Womb. *See* Uterus

Yohimbine, 44–45. *See also* Aphrodisiacs

Joann Ellison Rodgers, M.S. (Columbia), became the Deputy Director of Public Affairs and Director of Media Relations for the Johns Hopkins Medical Institutions in Baltimore, Maryland, in 1984 after 18 years as an award-winning science journalist and widely read columnist for the Hearst newspapers. She is the author of *Drugs and Pain* in the ENCYCLOPEDIA OF PSYCHOACTIVE DRUGS SERIES 2, published by Chelsea House.

Solomon H. Snyder, M.D., is Distinguished Service Professor of Neuroscience, Pharmacology and Psychiatry at The Johns Hopkins University School of Medicine. He has served as president of the Society for Neuroscience and in 1978 received the Albert Lasker Award in Medical Research. He has authored *Uses of Marijuana, Madness and the Brain, The Troubled Mind, Biological Aspects of Mental Disorder,* and edited *Perspective in Neuropharmacology: A Tribute to Julius Axelrod.* Professor Snyder was a research associate with Dr. Axelrod at the National Institutes of Health.

Barry L. Jacobs, Ph.D., is currently a professor in the program of neuroscience at Princeton University. Professor Jacobs is author of *Serotonin Neurotransmission and Behavior* and *Hallucinogens: Neurochemical, Behavioral and Clinical Perspectives.* He has written many journal articles in the field of neuroscience and contributed numerous chapters to books on behavior and brain science. He has been a member of several panels of the National Institute of Mental Health.